200
TIPS
for
CAKE
DECORATING

200 TIPS

for

CAKE
DECORATING
Tips, Techniques &
Trade Secrets

100+ BONUS tips!
Now, more than 300!

Carol
Deacon

FIREFLY BOOKS

A Firefly Book

Published by Firefly Books Ltd. 2013

First printing

Publisher Cataloging-in-Publication Data (U.S.)

Deacon, Carol.
200 tips for cake decorating : tips, techniques, and trade secrets / Carol Deacon.
[160] p. : col. photos. ;   cm.
Includes index.
Summary: Techniques for using fondant, butter cream, chocolate and marzipan to create cake decorations and edible delights. Topics include: cupcakes, cake pops, celebration cakes and more.
ISBN-13: 978-1-77085-202-0
1. Cake decorating. I. Title. II. Two hundred tips for cake decorating.
641.86 /539 dc23   TX771.2D433 2013

Library and Archives Canada Cataloguing in Publication

Deacon, Carol
        200 tips for cake decorating : tips, techniques, and trade secrets / Carol Deacon.
Includes index.
ISBN 978-1-77085-202-0
        1. Cake decorating. I. Title. II. Title: Two hundred tips for cake decorating.
TX771.2.D42 2013   641.86'539   C2013-900900-0

Published in the United States by
Firefly Books (U.S.) Inc.
P.O. Box 1338, Ellicott Station
Buffalo, New York 14205

Published in Canada by
Firefly Books Ltd.
50 Staples Avenue, Unit 1
Richmond Hill, Ontario L4B 0A7

Cover design: Erin R. Holmes/Soplari Design

Color separation in Singapore by Pica Digital Pte Ltd
Printed in China by 1010 Printing International Ltd

Conceived, designed, and produced by
Quarto Publishing plc
The Old Brewery
6 Blundell Street
London N7 9BH

For Quarto:
Project editor Chelsea Edwards; **Art editor and designer** Julie Francis; **Photographer** Philip Wilkins; **Illustrators** Hennie Haworth and John Woodcock; **Picture researcher** Sarah Bell; **Copyeditor** Lindsay Kaubi; **Proofreader** Claire Waite Brown; **Indexer** Helen Snaith; **U.S. consultant** Dianne Gruenberg; **Art director** Caroline Guest; **Creative director** Moira Clinch; **Publisher:** Paul Carslake

Contents

Foreword

I started cake decorating by accident—a friend needed a birthday cake and asked me to make one for her. It was an innocent enough request, but it sent me, piping bag in one hand, whisk in the other, down a path of sugary discovery. Much of what I learned was by trial and error since there was nothing like the amount of information and equipment around then that there is now. I kept on baking, and this book is a way of passing on some of that information. I hope that dipping in and out of these pages will take some of the effort and mystique out of the craft of cake decoration, and encourage many more of you to have a try.

Fondant wishes,

Carol Deacon

About this book

Suitable for any level of cake decorator from the professional to the beginner taking their first sticky steps into the world of cake decorating, this book contains over 300 hints, tips, expert secrets and problem-fixing solutions. Split into four chapters, the reader can use the succinct information and photographs to help with any cake decorating project.

Cake basics
(pages 8–39)

This chapter will guide you through selecting the right tools and equipment, baking the perfect base cake using the recipes provided and getting your cake ready for decorating.

Fondant
(pages 40–101)

This section deals with the tools that you will need to get you started, how to work with fondant and how to create wonderful fondant designs. It also deals with the basics of covering a cake and board with fondant. A portion of this chapter also deals with marzipan (almond paste). Although the taste of marzipan is totally different to that of fondant it can often be used in the same way.

Buttercream
(pages 102–125)

A simple but delicious buttercream recipe is essential for creating successful cakes. This chapter deals with making, flavoring, and covering both large cakes and cupcakes with buttercream. It also takes buttercream a stage further, showing the reader how to pipe lettering and flowers, create frozen buttercream transfers, and even make little piped animals and people.

Chocolate
(pages 126–143)

If you have ever wanted to create luscious chocolate decorations then this is the chapter for you. It will guide you through the tools that you need, the different types of chocolate and how to work it successfully to both cover cakes and create chocolate decorations. It also contains a tasty chocolate cake pop for using up leftover cake and a truffle recipe.

Tips
Tips are liberally sprinkled all through the book, and will offer shortcuts or alternative ways of achieving a great end result.

"Fix it" panels
These appear regularly throughout the projects and offer ways to solve problems or common pitfalls or repair damaged or spoiled projects.

Step-by-step sequences
Detailed step-by-step photographs and captions will teach you many exciting techniques, from the very basic first steps in cake decorating through to more complicated projects.

"Try it" panels
These panels appear throughout the book and their tricks and tips should inspire you to push your cake decorating further than you ever thought possible.

Recipes
Delicious cake and icing recipes are featured to help you create great-tasting, as well as great-looking cakes.

Finished Projects
Finished cake projects will inspire you with ways to implement new techniques and help you create your own designs.

1 Cake basics

This chapter deals with the start of the cake-making process, through baking the cake and preparing it for decoration. This section also explores cake presentation, stacking your cakes, decorating your cake boards, and how to use ribbons and candles to their best effect.

Essential equipment

At the most simple level, a bowl, spoon, pan, and an oven to bake your cake in are all that you need for the perfect base to decorate. Beyond this you will find a sifter, scales, and an electric mixer very useful. When it comes to decorating your cake there are simply so many gadgets and gizmos available that it can be tricky to know where to start. This section looks at the most useful tools for decorating with fondant, buttercream, and chocolate.

◀ Rolling pin
A rolling pin is essential for rolling out fondant to cover cakes and boards.

▲ Small, sharp nonserrated knife
A small, sharp knife is necessary for cutting through fondant. A nonserrated (smooth, not jagged) blade is best, because it should cut through the icing without pulling and tearing it.

▲ Palette knife
Used for spreading buttercream onto a cake ready for covering with fondant, or for applying fillings.

◀ Scissors
From cutting ribbons to removing excess fondant when modeling, a good, sharp pair of scissors is an invaluable tool.

▲ Wooden spoon
Wooden spoons can be used for beating your cake batters and frostings. As wood does not conduct heat, they are especially useful for stirring chocolate on the stove.

▲ Metal spoon
Useful for stirring chocolate and ladling products out of bags into scales, a plain metal spoon has many uses in the kitchen.

▲ Plastic spatula
This is necessary for effectively mixing your icing, especially when working with buttercream.

◀ Paintbrushes
A fine and a medium paintbrush will become essential parts of your kit. They should have soft tips that will not mark or dent the surface of the fondant. You will use these to stick your models together and "paint" patterns and messages on your cakes.

Sifter ▼
A sifter is inexpensive to buy and allows you to remove lumps and introduce air into your cake as you sift the flour into the batter.

▼ Measuring spoons
Available in metal or plastic, these can be used to measure out either liquid or dry ingredients. Usually the spoons come in four-spoon sets—tablespoon (15 ml), teaspoon (5 ml), $\frac{1}{2}$ teaspoon (2.5 ml), and $\frac{1}{4}$ teaspoon (1 ml).

▼ Handheld whisk
A handheld electric whisk takes all the effort out of beating cake or frosting ingredients together.

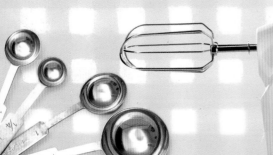

◄ Microwave

Not only is a microwave useful for melting chocolate and softening butter, fondant, and marzipan, it can also be used for tempering the chocolate.

Stovetop

It doesn't matter whether your stovetop runs on gas or electric. It simply needs to function correctly at a low heat so that you can gently simmer a pan of water on it while melting chocolate.

◄ Cake pans

The first decision to make is what size and shape your cake will be. There is a huge selection available.

◄ Measuring jug or cup

This is used to measure liquids that are to be added to your recipe. Always stand your measuring jug on a level surface to get an accurate measurement.

◄ Mixing bowls

You will need a good selection of glass and plastic bowls in various sizes. Bowls with lids are useful for storing batches of icing.

◄ Electric mixer

An electric mixer can cost the earth or be a simple, inexpensive handheld version. If you start making cakes on a regular basis it is worth investing in one to save your wrists from aching!

▼ Scales

A set of scales is a highly recommended tool. If you use cup measurements you may sometimes find your failsafe recipe failing for no apparent reason. Usually this is because the flour is slightly old; this means the oil in the flour may have dried out making the flour lighter. If the recipe is repeated using a set of scales, you may find that you actually need to use a larger volume of flour to achieve the weight of flour required by the recipe.

◄ Oven thermometer

Not every oven cooks accurately, so it's worth investigating if you are experiencing baking problems. Oven thermometers are not expensive. Just stand it inside the oven while it's on and check that the temperature on the dial matches that on the thermometer.

► Cooling rack

A cooling rack is a metal grid, usually with short legs. When you tip your freshly baked goodies out onto it, the air can circulate around the food allowing it to cool down more efficiently.

▲ Saucepan

You will need a saucepan for the water if you plan to melt chocolate on the stovetop. The size of your pan needs to allow your heatproof bowl to sit comfortably and securely on the top without touching the water in the pan.

▲ Heatproof bowl

You will need a deep bowl that can withstand sitting on top of a simmering saucepan of water. If you plan to melt chocolate using the microwave it must be microwave friendly too.

▼ Parchment paper or waxed paper

From making piping bags to creating templates and aiding with delicate piping work, these basics are must-haves.

Useful additional kit

These items, although not essential, can save time and help you achieve a more professional finish on your cakes. You don't need to buy everything at once, just add to your collection as you go along.

◀ Scraper

A scraper can be used to create smooth or textured effects in the buttercream on the top and sides of your cakes.

◀ Spacers

These are plastic strips that you can buy in various thicknesses. They are placed either side of the fondant or marzipan when you're rolling it out. They will stop the rolling pin from rolling the fondant thinner than the height of the spacers and ensure that the fondant is the same thickness all the way through.

▲ Dowels

Dowels are required to create a strong internal support system for tiered or stacked cakes that would otherwise collapse.

◀ Blossom plunge cutter

This is a useful tool for making tiny fondant flowers quickly and easily. Blossom plunge cutters often come in sets of three—one small ($1/4$ in/6 mm diameter), one medium ($3/8$ in/10 mm) and one larger one ($1/2$ in/13 mm). You will probably find that you use the middle-sized cutter the most, but having a couple of different size options is always useful.

Metal piping nozzle ▶

Even if you never go anywhere near a piping bag, a small nozzle will prove really useful. It doesn't matter what design it is, it's the large round base that is the important part. Use the nozzle to cut out small fondant circles for things such as flower centers. Hold the nozzle at an angle and press it into still-soft fondant to make scales on mermaid tails or smiles or frowns on fondant faces.

▲ Textured rolling pin

You can easily create an interesting texture on your fondant using this simple piece of equipment.

◀ Chocolate thermometer

If you think you might get serious about working with chocolate, then a food-friendly thermometer is vital. They are not terribly expensive. Obtaining certain temperatures is tremendously important with chocolate.

◀ Cheese grater

Instead of using a knife, many people prefer to grate chocolate to help it melt quickly and evenly.

Five-petal flower cutter ▼

There are thousands of flower cutters you can buy and create incredible blooms with; however, the simple five-petal cutter is one of the most useful. Use it to create bold and happy fondant flowers with a slightly cartoonish look. These cutters are available in a number of sizes and it is worth having at least two size variations to work with.

◀ Pizza cutter

The smooth motion of the circular pizza cutter blade makes cutting long strips of fondant easier and neater than if done using a knife. It can also be useful for trimming the excess fondant from around the bottom of a cake after covering it.

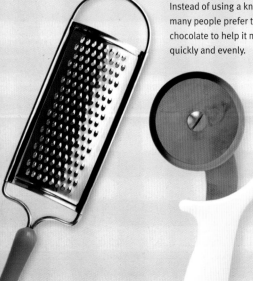

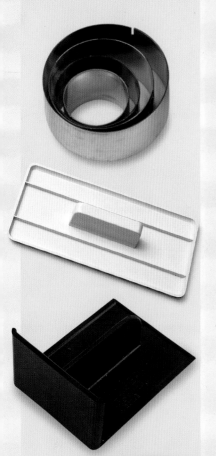

◀ Circle cutters

A set of circle cutters will prove invaluable, as many designs require a flat circular disk of icing somewhere in their construction. A set of cutters like this, in concentric circles, will reduce the frustrating alternative of rummaging around the kitchen looking for an appropriately sized lid when the design calls for a specific disk size. No one size is the "best" as the size required will depend on your design, but cutters ranging from $3/4$ in–$4^{1}/_{2}$ in diameters (2 cm–11 cm) are probably the most useful.

◀ Cake smoother

This is an ingenious tool that is simple to use but will transform your cakes. Holding the handle at the back, you smooth over the fondant surface of the cake. This will erase the lumpy look of a beginner's cake and produce the smooth, polished finish of a professional's.

Marble slab ▲

Used for tempering melted chocolate, a marble slab is ideal. If you don't have one, don't despair, there are alternative methods for bringing the temperature of chocolate down (see page 131).

◀ Edger

If you like to cover your cakes and boards with fondant all in one go, this tool will help you smooth the sides and the cake board at the same time.

Transfer sheets ▶

These sheets are used to transfer their design onto your cake or cookie. They are available in a huge range of colors and patterns so you can choose one that reflects the theme of your cake.

◀ Cake boards

These are available from cake decorating stores. They are available in a wide variety of colors and should only be used once.

▼ Chocolate molds

Chocolate molds for the amateur are available in all sorts of shapes, sizes, and designs. Made of plastic, they are fairly inexpensive, and if looked after, can be reused time and time again.

1

Keep your equipment dry

Always make sure your chocolate decorating equipment is clean and dry, never damp. Any hint of moisture will make the chocolate "seize" and become dry, gritty, and unusable in seconds.

Improvising tools

Walking into a cake decorating store and seeing how much equipment is now available to help you decorate cakes can be a daunting experience. Where on earth does a would-be cake decorator start?

Home tools

Although specialist equipment will undoubtedly improve the professional finish of your cakes, there are many items you probably have at home already that can be used to get you started. Once you're up and running simply buy the bits that you need as you go along.

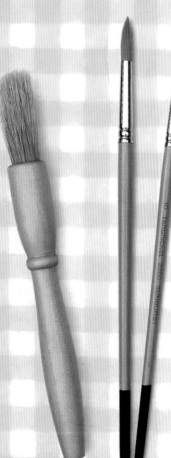

Toothpicks ▶
This simple kitchen tool can be used to add food color paste to fondant and is also useful for creating indents and markings on fondant models.

◀ Paintbrush
A soft paintbrush will become one of the most important items in your craft box. You will use it for lifting tiny bits of fondant into position on your models and making mouths and ears. You can also use a paintbrush on its side as a mini rolling pin.

◀ Wooden spoon
The rounded handle end of a wooden spoon can be used to make hollows in fondant models. Two laid flat together also make excellent drying formers if you need to make flags or bows.

Jar lids ▶
If you don't possess a set of circle cutters, collect a selection of different-sized lids instead. These are useful for cutting out fondant eyes, hats, spots, etc. You can also use them to cut out cookies or press scales into the sides of fondant dinosaurs, snakes, or mermaids' tails.

▲ Pastry brush
A large soft brush is useful for brushing and tidying up your models and also dabbing water onto large areas, such as cake boards before they are covered with fondant.

Bottle tops ▶
Use a bottle top to create the veins of a leaf.

Hard-bristled brush ▲

A scrubbing brush can be a great piece of cake decorating kit—use it to create texture and form on your cakes. You can create wispy clouds, frosted snow, or even sand grains for a holiday-themed cake!

▶ Scissors

As well as snipping off corners of sandwich bags for piping, you can use (clean) scissors to cut fondant. This technique is useful for making models such as fir trees or spiky hair.

Drinking straw ▶

Ah, the humble drinking straw: not only is it fantastic for sipping cool drinks through on a hot summer's day, but it can be used as a tiny circle cutter for making eyes, tiny "U" shaped smiles, cheeks, and eyebrows on your fondant characters.

Garlic press ▶

Stick a lump of fondant into a (washed!) garlic press and you can create the most amazing long strands to decorate your cakes and models. An essential tool for making hair, should you ever be asked to create an aging-hippie cake!

▲ Children's lettering

Once extracted from the toy box and given a good clean, children's lettering toys can be used to write messages on your cakes. Press them into soft fondant to leave an impression behind, or arrange them on top of the cake and remove when cutting.

Fondant strands using the garlic press ▶

Use fondant strands made with a garlic press to create hair for models or blades of green grass.

Cake recipes

No matter how good a cake looks on the outside, it needs to taste great on the inside too. The following recipes should help you to create cakes that are full of flavor and easy to work with.

Pound cake

This is a moist yet strong cake, which is extremely versatile and simple to make. It can be carved into shapes to delight the palates of a society wedding or even produce a fluffy cupcake. See opposite for how to make your own self-rising flour to use in this recipe. This cake is best eaten within a week. It can be frozen for up to 3 months.

INGREDIENTS

SQUARE PAN		6 in (15 cm)	7 in (18 cm)	8 in (20 cm)	9 in (23 cm)	10 in (25 cm)	11 in (28 cm)	12 in (30 cm)
ROUND PAN	6 in (15 cm)	7 in (18 cm)	8 in (20 cm)	9 in (23 cm)	10 in (25 cm)	11 in (28 cm)	12 in (30 cm)	
BUTTER	½ cup (120 g)	¾ cup (175 g)	1¼ cups (300 g)	1¾ cups (400 g)	2 cups (450 g)	2¼ cups (500 g)	2½ cups (550 g)	3 cups (700 g)
SUPERFINE SUGAR	½ cup (120 g)	¾ cup (175 g)	1¼ cups (300 g)	1¾ cups (400 g)	2 cups (450 g)	2¼ cups (500 g)	2½ cups (550 g)	3 cups (700 g)
SELF-RISING FLOUR	1½ cups (175 g)	2 cups (250 g)	2¾ cups (350 g)	3½ cups (450 g)	4 cups (500 g)	4½ cups (550 g)	5 cups (650 g)	6 cups (750 g)
EGGS	2	3	5	7	8	9	10	12
MILK	1 tbsp (15 ml)	1 tbsp (15 ml)	2 tbsp (30 ml)	3 tbsp (45 ml)	4 tbsp (60 ml)	5 tbsp (75 ml)	5 tbsp (75 ml)	6 tbsp (90 ml)
BAKING TIME (approx)	1 hr	1–1½ hrs	1½–2 hrs	1½–2¼ hrs	2 hrs	2 hrs	2–2½ hrs	2–2½ hrs

Method

1 Grease and line your cake pan (see page 18) and preheat your oven to 300°F (150°C).

2 If you are using a mixer, sift your flour into the bowl and add the rest of the ingredients. Mix on the slowest speed to gently bind the ingredients together. Switch to the mixer's highest speed and beat all the ingredients for a minute until the mixture is pale, smooth, and creamy.

If you are mixing by hand, make sure your butter is very soft (place it in a microwave for a few seconds if necessary). Then beat the butter and sugar together until creamy. Add the eggs and beat those in until the mixture is smooth. Sift the flour into the bowl and gently fold it in with a metal spoon, which is less likely to expel air.

3 Spoon the mixture into your prepared pan and smooth the top. Place the cake in the center of the preheated oven and bake for the required time. Not all ovens bake in the same way, so the baking times are approximate and you will need to check your cake. Your cake is ready when it is starting to pull away from the sides of the pan and you can't hear bubbling noises. To check, insert a knife or metal skewer. If it comes out clean then the cake is done. If there's mixture on the skewer, cook for another 5 minutes or so.

Make your own self-rising flour

Self-rising flour is used in many of the recipes shown here and is called different things in different countries. Very similar products are called self-raising or cake flour. Self-rising is flour that has a raising agent added to it to make your cakes lighter. You can make your own self-rising flour using a mixture of all-purpose flour (plain flour) and baking powder: Mix 1½ tsp (7 ml) of baking powder and 5½ oz or 1 cup (150 g) of all-purpose flour together. Double or triple these amounts if you need more for your recipe.

TRY IT

5 ADAPT THE RECIPE
You can easily adapt the pound cake recipe if you wish to. Stir in 1 tbsp (15 ml) of cocoa powder or coffee to produce a simple chocolate or coffee cake. You can also add a dash of flavoring, such as almond or mint, or stir in a mashed banana or the grated zest of an orange or lemon. You can alter the texture of the cake by adding a handful of dried coconut, raisins, chocolate chips, or chopped candied cherries.

Is my cake cooked?

A great way to test a cake to see if it is done is by pressing the center lightly. The surface should spring back if it is done. If it doesn't spring back, bake the cake for another 10 minutes and test again.

Work in batches

If you are making a big cake and don't possess a large mixing bowl, you may find it easier to halve the ingredients and mix them up in two portions. When ready, spoon the two batches into the prepared pan and stir them together.

TRY IT

7 ADD SOME COLOR
For a colorful surprise, stir in a little food coloring before baking. If you stir the coloring in lightly your cake will have a marbled appearance when cut. To achieve a solid color, mix the color in thoroughly.

▼ Coloring mixing
Food coloring can be mixed in thoroughly or lightly for varying effects.

Lining your cake pan

This is a key step in perfecting your cake base; you'll need to remove your cake intact from the pan in order to start the decorating stage. Here are a few ways to ensure your great-tasting cake comes out of the pan easily.

Waxed paper or parchment paper

This is the traditional method for lining a cake pan and will work for square, round, and other shaped pans with straight sides. Place the pan onto a sheet of waxed paper or parchment paper and draw around the base with a pencil. Using scissors, cut out the base shape.

1 Measure the circumference and height of the pan. Cut out a strip of paper a little wider than the height of the pan and a little longer than the circumference.

2 Make a fold about 1 in (2.5 cm) along one long edge of the strip and cut a fringe into it.

3 Lightly grease the pan by wiping a little solid shortening around it using a piece of paper towel. Although this is not essential it will hold the paper in place. Stand the edging strip inside the pan. The fringed base should splay and lie on the bottom of the pan. Then place the base section on top of the fringing in the bottom of the pan.

Paper liners

These come in various sizes and are already cut to size. You simply open the package and place one into the pan, add the cake batter, and bake.

Cooking sprays

These are especially useful if you're using an irregularly shaped pan that is impossible to line with waxed paper. Simply spray around the inside of the pan, fill with cake mixture, and bake.

Grease and flour

Before paper, sprays, and liners, this was the way baking pans were prepared. It's worth knowing about as an emergency standby method. Rub a little butter or solid shortening around the inside of the pan. Place a heaping tablespoon of flour into the pan and shake it around so it covers the inside of the pan. Place the cake batter inside and bake as usual.

Using stock syrup

This is a simple mixture of sugar and water that can be used to add extra moisture to your pound cakes.

To use the syrup, slice your pound cake into layers. Before filling, lightly dab the top of each layer with the cooled syrup using a soft pastry brush. Then fill your cake and assemble as usual. Just dab on the top if you're not layering your cake. Stock syrup can be stored in an airtight container in the refrigerator for 2 weeks (see recipe, right).

You can also use stock syrup for crystallizing fresh flowers with sugar (see page 94).

Stock syrup recipe

Ingredients
½ cup (120 g) granulated or super fine sugar
5 fl oz (150 ml) water

Method
Simply place the sugar and water into a saucepan and simmer gently for 5 minutes until the sugar has dissolved. Leave to cool before using.

TRY IT

11 FLAVORING STOCK SYRUP
You can flavor stock syrup with spirits or food essences. Simply add a splash to your desired strength. Here are some of the best flavor combinations:
• Rum works especially well with rich chocolate cake.
• Vanilla essence and lemon zest are great for livening up pound cake.

TRY IT

12 RELEASING YOUR CAKE
If you are worried that your cake will not come out cleanly from the pan, allow it to cool for 10 minutes before attempting to remove it. You will find that the cake has shrunk slightly as it has cooled, allowing you to easily free it from the pan. You can also try running a palette knife around the sides of the pan to help you remove the cake.

13

Fruitcake

Although the list of ingredients may look huge, making a fruitcake is not complicated. The secret is weighing everything out beforehand and allowing enough time to both put it together and for the cake to slowly bake. It is essential that the cake pan be properly lined to stop the sides from burning during the long cooking process.

INGREDIENTS

SQUARE PAN		6 in (15 cm)	7 in (18 cm)	8 in (20 cm)	9 in (23 cm)	10 in (25 cm)	11 in (28 cm)	12 in (30 cm)
ROUND PAN	6 in (15 cm)	7 in (18 cm)	8 in (20 cm)	9 in (23 cm)	10 in (25 cm)	11 in (28 cm)	12 in (30 cm)	
CURRANTS	½ cup (90 g)	1 cup (135 g)	1 heaping cup (175 g)	1½ cups (250 g)	1¾ cups (350 g)	2 cups (450 g)	3 cups (550 g)	4½ cups (700 g)
RAISINS	½ cup (90 g)	1 cup (135 g)	1 heaping cup (175 g)	1½ cups (250 g)	1¾ cups (350 g)	2 cups (450 g)	3 cups (550 g)	4½ cups (700 g)
SULTANAS (golden raisins)	½ cup (90 g)	1 cup (135 g)	1 heaping cup (175 g)	1½ cups (250 g)	1¾ cups (350 g)	2 cups (450 g)	3 cups (550 g)	4½ cups (700 g)
MIXED PEEL	¼ cup (20 g)	¼ cup (30 g)	⅓ cup (45 g)	½ cup (60 g)	½ cup (75 g)	¾ cup (100 g)	1 cup (120 g)	1½ cups (175 g)
CANDIED CHERRIES (halved)	⅓ cup (45 g)	⅓ cup (60 g)	½ cup (75 g)	1 cup (120 g)	1 cup (150 g)	1 cup (200 g)	1¼ cups (250 g)	1½ cups (300 g)
BRANDY	2 tbsp (30 ml)	2 tbsp (30 ml)	3 tbsp (45 ml)	4 tbsp (60 ml)	4 tbsp (60 ml)	6 tbsp (90 ml)	6 tbsp (90 ml)	8 tbsp (120 ml)
BUTTER	⅓ cup (90 g)	½ cup (135 g)	¾ cup (175 g)	1 cup (250 g)	1½ cups (350 g)	2 cups (450 g)	2½ cups (550 g)	3 cups (700 g)
SOFT BROWN SUGAR	½ cup (90 g)	¾ cup (135 g)	¾ cup (175 g)	1 cup (250 g)	2 cups (350 g)	2¼ cups (450 g)	3 cups (550 g)	3½ cups (700 g)
EGGS	2	3	4	6	8	10	12	15
ALL-PURPOSE FLOUR	¾ cup (90 g)	1 cup (135 g)	1⅓ cups (175 g)	2 cups (250 g)	2⅔ cups (350 g)	3¾ cups (450 g)	4⅓ cups (550 g)	5⅔ cups (700 g)
MIXED SPICE (apple pie spice)	½ tsp (2.5 ml)	½ tsp (2.5 ml)	1 tsp (5 ml)	1 tsp (5 ml)	2 tsp (10 ml)	2 tsp (10 ml)	3 tsp (15 ml)	3 tsp (15 ml)
CINNAMON	½ tsp (2.5 ml)	½ tsp (2.5 ml)	1 tsp (5 ml)	1 tsp (5 ml)	2 tsp (10 ml)	2 tsp (10 ml)	3 tsp (15 ml)	3 tsp (15 ml)
LEMON (zest only)	½ lemon	1 lemon	1 lemon	2 lemons	2 lemons	2 lemons	3 lemons	3 lemons
GROUND ALMONDS	¼ cup (20 g)	¼ cup (30 g)	⅓ cup (45 g)	⅓ cup (60 g)	¾ cup (75 g)	1 cup (100 g)	1¼ cups (120 g)	1½ cups (150 g)
FLAKED ALMONDS	¼ cup (20 g)	¼ cup (30 g)	⅓ cup (45 g)	⅓ cup (60 g)	¾ cup (75 g)	1 cup (100 g)	1¼ cups (120 g)	1½ cups (150 g)
BAKING TIME (approx)	1 hr	1½–2 hrs	2 hrs	2¼ hrs	2½ hrs	3 hrs	3 hrs	3 hrs

Lining the pan

The pan for a fruitcake needs to be double lined to provide extra protection for the cake as it bakes. Use the instructions for lining a pound cake (see page 18), but cut out four long strips and three base shapes. Stand two of the long strips around the outside of the pan and hold them in place with string tied into a knot (proper string—not plastic or it will melt!). Stand the other two long strips around the inside edges of the pan and place two of the base shapes into the bottom.

When you have made the mixture, spoon it into the prepared pan. Cut a small hole out of the center of the final base-sized shape and gently place it on top of the mixture. Don't press it down, it should simply rest on top and will prevent the cake from burning. The small hole will allow steam to escape.

Method

1 Line both the inside and outside of your cake pan and preheat the oven to 300°F (150°C).

2 Beat the butter and sugar together until they are soft and creamy. Then beat in the eggs one at a time.

3 Sift the flour and spices into the bowl and gently stir them in. If you are using a mixer, use the slowest speed. If you're mixing by hand, use a metal spoon. Then stir in the ground almonds. If the mixture looks too runny add a little more flour.

4 Stir the lemon zest and almonds into the dried fruit, then tip the fruits into the cake batter and mix together by hand.

5 Spoon the mixture into the prepared pan and gently smooth the top.

6 Place the disk of parchment paper with the hole cut out on the top of the mixture. Don't press it down, just let it lay on top.

7 Place the cake in the center of the preheated oven and bake. Remove the paper from the top of the cake about 15 minutes before it's finished baking. Lightly prod the top of the cake, if it feels very soft and you can still hear a lot of bubbling it is not cooked. If it looks done, feels firm to the touch and is silent, insert a skewer or sharp knife. If it comes out clean, the cake is ready. If it's not ready yet, bake it for another 5–10 minutes and test again. All ovens vary, so don't worry if yours cooks in a shorter or longer time than is suggested.

8 Allow the cake to cool completely in the pan before turning it out.

Storage and freezing

This cake can be kept for up to 3 months. Pierce the top a few times with a toothpick and drizzle a little brandy or fruit juice over the top. Tightly wrap the cake in two sheets of parchment paper then two sheets of aluminum foil and keep in a cupboard. You can "feed" the cake weekly with a little more brandy if you wish. Alternatively, the cake can be frozen undecorated and kept for up to 6 months.

14

Moisten your cake

For an extra-moist cake, place all the dried fruit into a bowl and cover, allowing them to soak overnight in 2 tbsp of brandy, or use fruit juice if you do not want to use alcohol. The fruits can soak like this for up to 2 days. Stir them occasionally.

TRY IT

15 MAKE A WISH!
If you are making this for use as a Christmas cake, let every member of the family have a chance to stir the raw mixture. Tell them to close their eyes as they mix and silently make a Christmas wish!

16

Be prepared

Your baking will run more smoothly if you have already weighed out the ingredients and gathered the right equipment before you start. Make sure you have allowed yourself enough time to finish the project. It's no use trying to produce a three-tier fruit wedding cake in half a day, for instance.

17

Chocolate cake

This excellent chocolate cake has a velvety texture that is easy to cut into regular shapes. It is essential that you have an electric mixer with a whisk attachment as well as a normal beater to make this. If you don't possess one, use the pound cake recipe (see page 16), but add some cocoa powder to it.

INGREDIENTS

SQUARE PAN		6 in (15 cm)	7 in (18 cm)	8 in (20 cm)	9 in (23 cm)	10 in (25 cm)	11 in (28 cm)	12 in (30 cm)
ROUND PAN	6 in (15 cm)	7 in (18 cm)	8 in (20 cm)	9 in (23 cm)	10 in (25 cm)	11 in (28 cm)	12 in (30 cm)	
BUTTER	⅓ cup (90 g)	½ cup (120 g)	¾ cup (175 g)	1 cup (250 g)	1¼ cups (300 g)	1½ cups (350 g)	1¾ cups (400 g)	2 cups (450 g)
SUPERFINE SUGAR	¼ cup (45 g)	⅓ cup (75 g)	½ cup (120 g)	⅔ cup (150 g)	¾ cup (175 g)	1 cup (200 g)	1 cup (250 g)	1⅓ cups (275 g)
EGGS, separated (medium)	3	4	6	8	10	12	14	16
PLAIN CHOCOLATE (semisweet)	5 oz (150 g)	6 oz (175 g)	8 oz (250 g)	10 oz (300 g)	12 oz (350 g)	14 oz (400 g)	1 lb (450 g)	1 lb 2 oz (500 g)
CONFECTIONERS' SUGAR	¼ cup (30 g)	⅓ cup (45 g)	½ cup (60 g)	⅔ cup (90 g)	¾ cup (100 g)	1 cup (130 g)	1 cup (150 g)	1⅓ cups (175 g)
SELF-RISING FLOUR	⅔ cup (90 g)	1 cup (120 g)	1¼ cups (175 g)	1¾ cups (250 g)	2¼ cups (300 g)	2¾ cups (350 g)	3¼ cups (400 g)	3¾ cups (450 g)
BAKING TIME (approx)	45 mins	45 mins–1 hr	1 hr	1–1¼ hrs	1–1¼ hrs	1¼–1½ hrs	1¼–1¾ hrs	1¼–2 hrs

Method

1 Preheat your oven to 350°F (180°C). Line your cake pan using one of the methods shown in the pound cake section (see page 18).

2 Separate the eggs, placing the whites and yolks in to two different bowls.

3 Melt the chocolate in a large heatproof bowl and place to one side.

4 Using the beater on your mixer, beat the butter and sugar together until fluffy.

5 Add the egg yolks to the mixture and beat them in too.

6 Tip the chocolate into the mixture. Scrape as much out as you can. Place the bowl that the chocolate was melted in to one side but don't dispose of it just yet. Mix the melted chocolate into the batter on a low speed.

7 Sift and gently stir the flour into the chocolate mixture using a metal spoon.

8 Scrape the chocolate mixture out of your mixing bowl into the melted chocolate bowl. Remove the beater from the mixer and wash and dry the mixing bowl.

9 Put the whisk attachment onto your mixer and place the egg whites into the cleaned mixing bowl. Whisk the egg whites until they're stiff, then add the confectioners' sugar and whisk that in too.

10 Remove the whisk and put the beater back onto your mixer.

11 Scrape the chocolate mixture into the egg whites and mix the two together on a slow speed. It may take a minute or two, but they will mix smoothly together eventually.

12 Pour the cake mixture into the prepared pan and bake immediately.

13 When the cake is ready it should be silent—no bubbling noises. To be absolutely sure, insert a knife or metal skewer (you may have to cut a small chunk out of the cake's crust to do this). If it comes out clean then the cake is done. If there's mixture on the skewer, cook for a little longer.

Storage and freezing
If you are not going to decorate the cake immediately, wrap it in plastic wrap once it has cooled until required. It should be eaten within 5 days.

Work in batches
Unless you have a very big mixer, it may be easier to make the largest cake sizes in two separate batches then gently stir together. Have everything weighed out beforehand as this mixture needs to be cooked immediately.

FIX IT

18 USE A THERMOMETER
Despite what it may say on the dial, not all ovens cook at accurate temperatures. If your cakes are sinking or burning it may mean that your oven is cooking at too high or too low a temperature. Invest in an oven thermometer—they are not particularly expensive—and place it in the oven to check the temperature is correct.

19 SLICE OFF THE CRUST
Often when this cake bakes a hard crust forms on top, and it may scorch or crack. Although it sounds odd, this is perfectly normal! Once the cake has cooled and you're ready to decorate it, simply slice the crusty bits off and discard them. See page 26 for the best way to do this.

▶ In the mix
The benefits of a mixer stretch far beyond just baking. You'll find they're useful for mixing up icing and fondant recipes.

20

Go with the flow

Make sure that you don't place one cake pan above another in the oven. An even flow of heat is important and crowding cake pans into the oven will hinder the flow and result in disappointing cakes.

21

Work in advance

Remember, you can easily freeze this cake, so you could bake it well in advance of an important occasion when timing isn't so pressured. Allow the cake to cool and cover with plastic wrap before freezing. Eat within 3 months.

22

Calculating mixture quantities for unusual cakes

At some point, you may be faced with trying to calculate how much cake mixture you will need for a very large or very small pan, or even an unusually shaped novelty cake pan. While you could simply double the quantities for a favorite recipe, there is a more scientific method to use if you don't want to incur any waste.

Large pans

1 Fill a cake pan that you have used before—and for which you know the quantity of cake mixture needed—two-thirds full of water (two-thirds because that's how much mixture you would normally pour in.)

2 Tip the water into the pan that you are planning to use.

3 Repeat, counting the number of times you need to do it until the new pan is two-thirds full.

4 If the number of times you need to pour water into the pan is double the number needed to fill your usual pan, then you know that you need to make double the amount of cake mixture. If the larger pan takes three times as much, triple the amount of cake mixture you make.

Smaller pans

1 Fill the small pan that you plan to use two-thirds full with water.

2 Tip this water into a pan that you have used before and for which you know the quantity of cake mixture needed.

3 Continue to tip water from the smaller pan into the larger pan until the larger one is two-thirds full.

4 If you had to empty the small pan three times then you know you need to make one-third of the amount of cake mixture that you would use for the bigger one, so divide the quantities by three.

23

Seasoning your pans

New pans should be seasoned properly before using for the first time to ensure the easy release of the cake after baking. Apply a thin coat of solid shortening to the sides and bottom of the pan. Place the pan in a 150°F–200°F (65°C–95°C) oven for 30–45 minutes. If there are specific instructions that came with the pan, follow them.

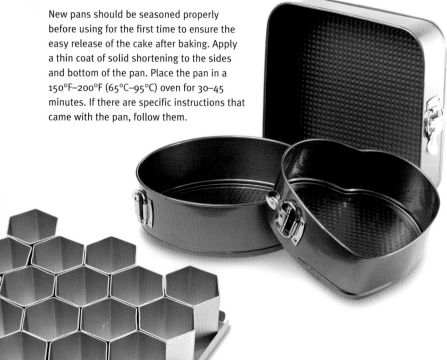

FIX IT

24
HELP! MY CAKES KEEP SINKING IN THE MIDDLE
If you find that your cakes are sinking in the middle, it could be because you are opening the oven door too early. The sudden flow of cold air onto a hot, uncooked cake is a recipe for a sinking disaster.

◀ **Pan out**
You don't need a complete range of pan sizes. You can always cut a small cake out of a larger one. Or stick two smaller cakes together to make a larger one.

25

How to fill cupcake liners neatly

The easiest way to spoon cake mixture into liners without getting too sticky is to use two teaspoons. Use the first one to scoop a dollop of batter out of the bowl. Then use the second to push it off the first spoon into the cupcake liner.

Another useful tool for filling cupcake liners is a scoop. A 3-tbsp scoop (45 ml) is perfect for a standard-sized liner.

1 Preheat the oven to 300°F (150°C) and place your cupcake liners into the baking tray. Mix up the pound cake mixture (see page 16).

2 Spoon the mixture into the cupcake liners. Fill each liner to about two-thirds full. Take care with this, if you add too much mixture they'll burst their liners and spread over the pan. Bake for about 25 minutes until the cakes are golden and springy to the touch.

▲ **Presentation pieces**
Tiny candies make great cucpcake and table decorations, giving the impression of confetti.

26

Cupcake cones

If you want to display your cupcakes in a fun and different way, why not use an ice-cream cone? Trim down the sides of your baked cupcake and gently slide it into the cone. Finish the iced cupcake with a chocolate stick—great for summer parties.

27

Making cupcakes

There are dozens of recipes available for cupcakes, but the pound cake recipe on page 16 is an easy-to-make recipe that will produce great results. If you use the amounts given for the two-egg mixture, you should be able to make about 12 cupcakes. If you want more, simply double or triple the quantities. To add a little fun to your cupcakes you could add some chocolate chips, a handful of dried fruit, a spoonful of cocoa powder or even a dash of food coloring.

Preparing the perfect cake

Once your cake is baked and cooled, the next step is to prepare it for decoration. In the unlikely event that your cake performed less than perfectly in the oven, these simple hints will help you achieve an elegant and professional finish.

▲ A cut above
A cake that has cracked, scorched or simply risen too high is still edible. Simply slice the offending sections off.

 28

Leveling the cake

Most cakes will rise when they are cooking in the oven and form a domed shape. Although there is nothing wrong with this homely and informal effect, most cake designs require a flat surface. There are several ways to achieve this.

Slicing the top off

It sounds obvious, and it is! Always make sure that you are using a clean, sharp carving knife and, holding it flat and level, gently slice the top of the cake off. If the cake is not too large and is firm enough, you may find it easier to place it on its side to do this.

Turn it upside down

If, once you have removed most of the domed top, your cake is still not flat enough, then simply turn it upside down. What was once the base will now become a nice flat top.

Using a cake leveler

A cake leveler is a "U"-shaped piece of metal designed to sit over the cake. It has a thin wire or blade that stretches between the two sides of its handle, much like a large cheese wire. Holding it vertically, you slide it through the cake to produce a neat, flat cut. Levelers are usually adjustable so that you can cut the cake easily into horizontal slices.

 29

Removing the crust

As well as leveling the cake it is common practice on special occasion cakes, such as wedding cakes, to remove the dark crust from around the sides, base and top of the cake. This will mean the cake looks "clean" when cut. Simply slice the outside crust off with a clean, sharp carving knife and discard.

If you know that you will be removing the crust around the sides, bake a larger-sized cake than you actually require. Although the cake may look prettier once you have cut the crust off, you will be left with a smaller cake than the one you baked.

FIX IT

30 RAGGED SLICING
To get a really clean cut through your cake, allow it to sit for a day so that it firms up. It will slice far more cleanly than a freshly cooled cake.

31

Leveling a fruitcake

The domed top of a fruitcake will normally be sliced off and removed and the cake turned upside down onto a cake board, in the same way as for a pound cake, but the similarities end there.

You then need to check the fruitcake for any "holes" and plug these with small balls of marzipan. This will level the cake out and make for an even surface to cover. If there is a gap between the board and the base of the cake, press a sausage of marzipan into the gap and trim to fit. Pierce the top of the cake a few times with a toothpick and drizzle a little brandy over the top for a bit of extra moisture. Boil 3 tbsp (45 ml) of apricot jam and "paint" it over the top and sides of the cake using a pastry brush. The fruitcake is now ready to be covered with marzipan.

TRY IT

32 BAKE A STRIPY CAKE
To give your guests a stripy surprise, try baking contrasting color cakes. You could do this with chocolate and plain sponge or add food coloring to different batters. Slice the cakes into layers, but reassemble them into one cake with alternating layers. When the cake is cut, the slices will be striped.

33

Baking a tall cake

If you want to produce a towering layer cake, the trick is to bake two or three cakes and stack them on top of each other, rather than attempting to bake one very deep cake.

34

Torting the cake

Once your cake has been leveled, it will usually need to be sliced into horizontal layers (known as torting) ready to be spread with the fillings of your choice.

Torting at a stroke
You can simply slice the cake carefully into two or three layers using a large carving knife, but this may mean that the layers are not completely straight. While this would not be a problem in some circumstances, it might be distressing for a bride and groom when captured for posterity in a wedding photo. An adjustable cake leveler is the best implement to use for cutting layers, provided the cake is not too large (see opposite).

Turn to a turntable
Place your cake on its board onto a turntable. Holding it flat, press the tip of a sharp knife into the side of your cake and rotate the turntable once. You should now have a straight line around the side of the cake. Using a carving knife, cut across the cake using a light sawing motion, keeping to the line around the sides. You should then be able to remove the top layer. Repeat a second time if you are cutting your cake into three layers.

▲ **Torting with a turntable**
A turntable will prove to be worth its weight in gold in all aspects of cake decorating, including the simple act of torting your cake.

Working on a small scale

Not all cake designs have to be huge affairs. Indeed, there is something very personal (and time-consuming!) about making small individual cakes for your guests. They could be as simple as a happy little cupcake or as complicated as a sophisticated, ornately piped mini fruitcake.

▲ **Small-scale pans**
If you decide to downsize your cake decorating, do not be concerned about limited pan options. There is an abundance of tiny tins and trays to choose from.

 35

Picking pans

There are so many options when it comes to small-scale pans. Here are some of the most useful:

Mini pans
If you are making a batch of mini cakes, you can buy sets of mini cake pans. These come in various shapes—for example, circular, square, and hexagonal, to name a few. In addition they are available in different materials, namely metal and silicone. Cakes bake well in both types so it's a question of personal preference, although silicone has the advantage of being able to be used in the microwave. The initial outlay might be expensive, but they can both be used over and over again to ensure you get your money's worth.

Cake trays
Cupcake, muffin, or other ornate cake trays can also be used to produce mini cakes. Bake the pound cake mix then decorate with buttercream, fondant, or chocolate.

Cutout cakes
If you require a number of small cakes of a certain size but you don't possess a baking pan in the right size, bake some large flat cakes (a roasting pan is useful for this) and cut your cakes out using a cutter.

 36

Preparing cupcakes

Let's start with everybody's favorite: the cupcake. Once a cupcake is baked, there is very little preparation to be done before the cake is ready to be decorated. If the top has risen too much or singed slightly you may wish to slice a little off to make a flatter base, or to remove any possible hint of a burned taste.

 37

Baked bean cake pans

Baked bean cans make excellent small cake pans. To use, place a washed out can onto some parchment paper and trace around the base. Cut out the resulting disk. Measure the height and circumference of the can and cut out a strip of parchment slightly taller than its height and longer than its circumference. Stand the strip around the inside of the can and place the disk in the base. Fill the can two-thirds full of cake mixture and bake.

38

Mini wedding cake

Many couples prefer to break with tradition and opt for a tower of cupcakes or mini cakes rather than the traditional tiered wedding cake. An abundance of these delicate iced love hearts would also look beautiful. Change the ribbon color to match the wedding color scheme.

1 Use paper towel to wipe a little solid shortening around the inside of each heart-shaped pan. To further aid in removing each cake from the pan, cut out a small disk of baking paper and lay it in the base of each heart.

2 Fill each heart approximately two-thirds full with the cake mixture. Bake in the oven at 300°F (150°C) for between 20–30 minutes. Remove from the oven when golden and springy to the touch. Turn out and cool on a cooling rack. Remove the paper disks.

3 When ready to decorate, split a heart in half horizontally and sandwich together with buttercream and jam. Place onto a board and coat the outside of the heart with buttercream too.

4 Lightly dust your work surface with confectioners' sugar. Knead and roll out 2 oz (60 g) of white fondant. Roll no thinner than ¼ in (5 mm).

5 Lift and place over the cake. Smooth it into position and trim away the excess from around the base with a small, sharp knife. Repeat on the other heart cakes.

6 Finish off by piping a "snail trail" of royal icing around the base of the cake (see page 117) and pipe a few dots onto the surface of the cake. Tie a small bow and attach to the cake with a little royal icing or a blob of wet, sticky fondant.

39

Make your own cutter template

If you don't have a cutter of the appropriate size or shape, you can improvise by cutting out a template from a cereal box and cutting around that instead.

▼ DIY templates
Here are some shapes you can trace and cut out to make your own templates.

Hidden surprises

It may look like an ordinary cupcake from the outside, but slice it open and you'll find a little colored cake surprise inside. These would be ideal for serving at a baby shower to reveal if it's a boy or a girl. Use foil or silicone cake liners so nothing can be seen from the outside and decorate the top with thick neutral buttercream. Use blue circles for a boy and pink for a girl.

1 Stir a little food coloring into some raw pound cake mixture. Bake it in a flat tray and allow it to cool.

2 Make a second batch of plain pound cake mixture and place the cupcake liners into the baking tray.

FIX IT

41 SHORT OF A CUTTER? If you don't have a circle cutter, cut the colored cake into cubes or improvise with a cardboard template (see page 29) instead.

3 Using a cutter, cut out your colored circular shapes.

4 Stand a cooked cake circle upright in the center of a cupcake liner and carefully spoon a little cake mixture on either side of the circle, and a little on top too.

5 Bake for about 15 minutes or until the cupcakes are golden and firm.

6 Allow to cool completely, then decorate.

◄ **The desired effect**
This is what will be revealed to your baby-shower guests, making the delivery of the news all that more interesting.

Cake pops

A cake pop is a mixture of crumbled cake and buttercream or chocolate. It's rolled into a ball shape, placed onto a lollipop stick and decorated. There are many ways of making a cake pop, but here's one of the simpler methods.

Simple buttercream cake pops
You can use a combination of buttercream and any type of cake, such as pound, chocolate, or coffee.

Crumble the cake into a bowl and weigh it. Then, weigh out the same amount of buttercream. So, if you have 4 oz (120 g) of crumb for example, you will need 4 oz (120 g) of buttercream. The pops can be eaten plain or dipped into some melted chocolate and sprinkles.

1 Mix the buttercream into the cake crumb.

2 Take a small handful and roll it into a ball shape.

3 Melt some chocolate (see page 129) and then dip the tip of your lollipop stick into the melted chocolate. This will act as glue when you poke it into the cake pop ball.

4 Melted chocolate is a great base for decorations to adhere to, so dip your pop into some melted chocolate. Either stand the pop on a baking tray to set or, if you don't want the pops to lose their rounded shape, push the sticks into a colander or a polystyrene block to firm up before decorating.

◄ Improvised stand
If you don't have a cake pop stand, you can improvise simply by using an upturned colander.

Stacking cakes

Whether making a tiered cake for a wedding or for an elaborate birthday cake, dowels can be used as the secret supports to bear the weight of the stacked cakes of your grand design.

▶ Perfect pillars
Choose a pillar color that matches or complements the base color of your cake.

◀ Aiming high
Pillars will add both height and drama to your cakes.

 43

Using pillars

The wedding pillar is the traditional method of standing one cake upon another. There are various pillar designs so use whichever you are most comfortable with. The basic method involves the use of cake pillars and dowels (long, thin, food-safe plastic rods). They must be placed equidistant both from each other and the edge of the cake.

1 Place each of your fondant-covered cakes on their own cake board. Using a tape measure, mark where you want the centers of the pillars positioned on the cake. Use a food color pen to do this.

2 Push pieces of dowel straight down into the cake until they reach the cake board.

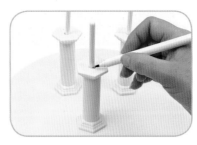

3 Place pillars over the top of the dowels. Using a pen, make a mark on the dowel, level with the top of the pillar.

4 Remove the pillar and carefully pull the dowel out of the cake. Using a serrated knife, partially saw across the pen mark. Bend and snap the dowel.

5 Insert the dowels back into the cake and place the pillars over the top. The top of the dowels should be level with the top of the pillars. When ready, place the cakes on top of each other.

Calculating pillar positions

This diagram shows you how to work out where to position pillars on a round cake, but the principles involved for most cake shapes are the same. Templates can be made from parchment paper or cardstock. To obtain a good shape in either case, either draw around the cake pan and cut out the shape just inside the line to allow for the thickness of the pan, or make a paper pattern following the instructions (see right). You can use either three or four pillars, it's just a matter of deciding which looks best.

Size of cake	Distance of pillar from center
8 in (20 cm)	2½ in (6.5 cm)
10 in (25 cm)	3 in (7.5 cm)
12 in (30 cm)	3½ in (9 cm)
14 in (35 cm)	4 in (10 cm)

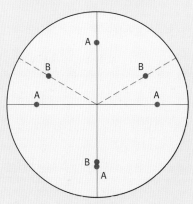

A round cake can either have four pillars on the cross (A) or three pillars on the triangle (B). For the cross, fold into four, open, and mark points (A) on the folds. For the triangle, fold in half and mark the first position (B) the correct distance from the center of the cake according to the chart (see left). Fold into three making an angle of 60°, and mark the second position (B) on the outside fold; open up and mark the third point (B) on the third fold. These same principles can be applied to most cake shapes.

Positioning pillars

The exact position of the pillars will depend on the size of the top tier, the board it will be sitting on and also the display of flowers or decoration that will be on it. The instructions here can be used as a guideline for positioning pillars—but a lot will depend upon the design of the cake.

1 Take a tracing of the surface of the coated cake using a sheet of baking parchment, fold the template into quarters (if using four pillars) and mark the distance of the pillars from the center of the cake.

2 Unfold the template and position it on top of the cake. Scribe the position of each pillar onto the icing. Now you have the correct position marked out for your four pillars.

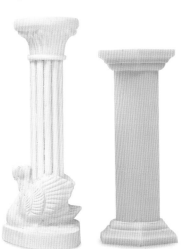

◄ Hard times
Whichever style of pillar you deicide to use you should let the fondant on the cake harden overnight before putting the pillars in place. That way you're less likely to dent and damage the surface of the fondant.

46

Using cake boards for decoration

It is now possible to buy cake boards in different colors, and they can be used as colorful three-dimensional supports or display bases for your designs even without being covered. Gold foil boards work well with chocolate, but there's a whole range of colors for you to choose from.

47

Fake tiers

Dummy cakes are polystyrene blocks that come in all sorts of shapes and sizes, allowing you to create an elegant-looking cake without having to bake endless layers of cake. Simply cover them in fondant.

48

Using cake boards for support

A thin cake board standing vertically at the rear of a cake can be used to provide support for standing fondant figures, or can act as a background. It can be decorated so that it becomes part of the design, and it will mean that you do not have to put supports inside the figures.

1 Cover the entire board with fondant using the method shown on page 54.

2 Stand it against the back of the cake and make a mark level with the top of the cake. The decorations on the board must not go below this mark.

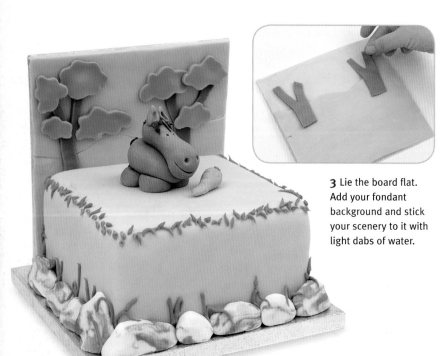

3 Lie the board flat. Add your fondant background and stick your scenery to it with light dabs of water.

4 Stand the decorated board against the cake and stick it into place with dabs of royal icing or lumps of very wet and sticky fondant. (Dip the fondant in water and knead it to make it extra sticky.)

49

Internal supports

Stacked cakes without pillars have grown in popularity and can give a design a modern, contemporary feel. As with the traditional pillars (see page 32), the secret behind (or should that be "beneath"?) the successful stacking of this style of cake is the humble plastic cake dowel.

◄ **Stacking up**

Using this system you can stack cakes as high as you want.

1 Beginning with the base cake, carefully push three or four cake dowels vertically into the center of the cake in a square or triangular formation. They must reach right down to the board and be equidistant from each other and the edge of the cake. Using a food color pen, make a mark on each dowel level with the top of the cake.

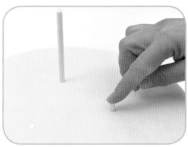

2 Carefully pull out one of the dowels. Using a serrated knife partially saw across the pencil mark, and then bend and snap the dowel. Insert the dowel back into the cake. The top of the dowel must be level with the top of the cake. Repeat with the other dowels.

3 Spread a little royal icing between the dowels. This will act as "glue" to hold the cake above in place.

4 Place the next cake into position on top of the first using a fish slice or large spatula. This way you are less likely to get finger marks on the fondant.

5 You can neaten the seams by piping around the bases of the cakes with additional royal icing. Once set, the royal icing will also stop the cakes from moving when you travel with them to their destination.

► **Hiding the seams**

The seams are hidden on this design by strands of fondant individually stuck around the sides of the cake. You can achieve a similar effect by using a number 7 piping nozzle.

50

Stacking cake boards for cupcake displays

Although the world seems full of cupcake display stands, there may come a time when you need something very simple or themed to a particular color. This is a way of creating your own stand. You will need small polystyrene cake dummies or blocks. You can buy these from most cake decorating equipment stores.

You can display cakes on either a single board or arrange them in a tiered group. To create a smooth, neat look, ensure that the size difference between each of the boards is the same. For instance use a 10-in (25 cm), 12-in (30 cm), and 14-in (35 cm) board or 8-in (20 cm), 12-in (30 cm), and 16-in (40 cm) boards.

◀ **Flower power**
When making your stand, use colors that complement the cakes it will be displaying.

1 First you need to cover each board with a thin coating of fondant. To do this use the technique shown on page 54.

2 Stick a piece of ribbon around the edge of each board and secure in place with a nontoxic glue stick or some double-sided tape.

3 Wrap ribbon around the two polystyrene cake dummies and glue in place using a nontoxic glue stick or double-sided tape.

4 Stick one of the ribbon-covered columns in the center of the biggest board with a generous dab of royal icing.

5 Spread some royal icing on the top of the column and place the middle board on top.

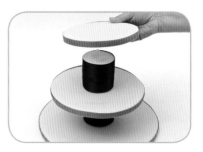

6 Stick the second column in the middle of the second board and stick the final board in place on top. Allow the display stand to dry overnight before filling with cupcakes.

51

Use textured fondant

Your tasty cupcakes won't stick around for long on their beautiful display board, so why not make sure what's left behind still looks lovely? You can do this by texturing the fondant you use to cover your display boards (see page 57).

52

Heavy decorations

Cake centerpieces, such as elaborate fondant cake toppers, models, or candles, can be heavy. To stop the decoration squashing your cake, consider making the model on a thin cake card. This will disperse the weight across the cake.

For extra support you can also use a single plastic cake dowel. Push the dowel into the cake right down to the board and make a mark where it's level with the top of the cake. Remove the dowel and partially cut across it with a serrated knife. Bend and snap the dowel and reinsert the measured section back into the cake. The top of the dowel should be level with the top of the cake. Now simply place the decoration on its board on top.

54

Candles

A birthday cake wouldn't be a birthday cake without candles! You can choose from an incredible array of designs and colors to get the look you want. As well as tall and elegant, chubby and cheerful candles there's a plethora of novelty candles. Some even make music or burst into firework-type sparkles. It is worth spending a few minutes thinking about whether or not adding candles will enhance your design, rather than just including them regardless.

55

Candleholders

It is easy to make your own candleholders, which can then form part of your design. Fondant and marzipan are both especially good for this. Why not use one of the fondant models from pages 79–86 as a candleholder? You can make your model look as though it is holding the candle in place.

TRY IT

56
FLOWERY CANDLEHOLDERS
Roll a little colored fondant out, keeping it thick, no thinner than $1/4$ in (5 mm). Cut out a flower shape using a flower cutter. Stick the flower onto the cake and insert a candle into its center.

◀ **Fire safety**
Make sure the candle is pushed securely into the candleholder before pushing it into the model.

Using ribbons

Ribbons have been used as decoration on cakes for centuries, and even nowadays a cleverly chosen ribbon can enhance a design.

57

Wrapping your cake

If you just wish to stand a ribbon around the side of a cake, measure the circumference first using a tape measure and add an extra inch (2.5 cm) to the length to allow for the seam. You can secure the seam at the back of the cake in a number of ways:

- Use a piece of clear sticky tape to hold the overlapping ends of the ribbon in place. The tape should not touch the cake's surface.
- Use a dab of buttercream or royal icing to "glue" the ends in place.
- Dip a little fondant into water and work it in with your fingers until it is gooey and sticky, then use it to join the two ends.

58

Ribbon weaving

This is a very old technique that gives the appearance of ribbon having been threaded through the cake and works particularly well on christening and baby cakes. Ribbon insertions work best on a fondant-covered cake. This is because as you cut into it there are no oils to bleed into the ribbon, unlike with buttercream. The ideal point to try this technique at is when the fondant has crusted over slightly, but has not become solid. You will need a scalpel or a very sharp craft knife, a dressmaker's pin, and a pair of scissors. Tweezers are also useful if you are handling tiny sections of ribbon.

1 Holding your knife vertically, cut a couple of small slits, the width of the ribbon you intend to use, into the fondant.

2 Cut a number of short sections of ribbon. The ribbon lengths should be slightly longer than the distance between the slits on the cake so that the ribbon can form an attractive loop and also tuck into the fondant.

3 Gently push each end of a section of ribbon into two cuts in the fondant. Use the pin to carefully poke it in. Once done the ribbon should stay in place.

◄ All tied up
The result is a versatile design, suitable for many different occasions.

Beautiful bows

If you want to add a bow to the ribbon around the cake it is best to make it out of a separate section of ribbon. This reduces the chances of you damaging the sides of the cake when you pull the ribbon taut to tie the bow. Make a bow and stick it in place with either a dab of royal icing or a sticky blob of dipped fondant. Alternatively, you could use a little double-sided tape, but make sure the tape does not come into contact with the surface of the cake.

60

Liven up a cake pop

Once you've created your wonderful and tasty cake pops you want to make sure they're presented attractively. If you want to serve your pops on a plate you can decorate the pop sticks with little ribbon bows, tying the colors in with your table settings.

61

Dressing a board

If you are making an important cake, such as a wedding cake, you might wish to cover the edges of the board with ribbon. Measure the height of the board edge and choose ribbon with a width as close to that measurement as possible. You can attach the ribbon to the board in two ways:

Glue
You can use a nontoxic glue stick to stick the ribbon around the edge of the board. Test it first on a section of ribbon to make sure it does not bleed through and make sure the glue does not come into contact with any icing on the top of the cake board. Conceal the seam by placing it at the back of the cake.

Double-sided tape
Cut a number of small sections of double-sided tape and stick them around the edges of the board. Remove the protective top layer and, starting from the back of the cake, stick the ribbon in place. By starting there you will ensure the seam is at the back of the cake.

62

Fondant ribbon

If you like the look of ribbon weaving (see opposite), but want to use fondant instead, this is perfectly achievable. Roll a thin strip of colored fondant the width of silk ribbon. Cut the pieces evenly in lengths the same size as you would have done for the ribbon technique. Bend each piece of fondant over a wooden dowel and allow to dry. It's a good idea to make more than you'll need to allow for breakages. You can add a touch of shimmer dust to give it the look of ribbon. When the fondant lengths are dry, use tweezers to insert the fondant ribbon into the slits of fondant on the cake. The fondant covering must be soft for this to work.

2 Fondant

Fondant, sometimes called sugarpaste, is a thick, sweet dough, which can be used in a similar way to edible modeling clay. It is an extremely versatile type of icing, and may also be called ready-to-roll icing, plastic icing, and rolled fondant. Fondant can be used to both cover cakes and to make models and shapes, and it is extremely easy to use, which makes it suitable for anyone to work with, including children and beginners.

Fondant varieties

Throughout this book, "fondant" refers to the sweet, dough-like, edible modeling icing, sometimes called sugarpaste or rolled fondant. However, you may also come across "poured fondant," which is a liquid substance great for covering cakes, but not suitable for modeling.

▶ **Covering up**
Following a few simple rules will give your cakes a perfect covering.

Make your own fondant

If you prefer to make your ingredients from scratch, you can make your own fondant, but be warned, it is a messy procedure. These recipes should produce enough fondant to cover an 8 in (20 cm) round cake. Making any more than this in one session will require an enormous industrial mixer with a dough hook! Therefore it is easier to mix up small quantities and knead them together when ready.

Buying fondant

Thanks to the increase in popularity of cake decorating over the past few years, ready-made fondant is widely available from cake decorating stores, online stores and larger supermarkets. All will perform in a similar way, but there may be a slight difference in taste between brands. The advantages of using store-bought fondant are the time it saves and its consistency, which will always be the same.

Fondant recipe

This recipe is simple to put together. Liquid glucose is available from cake stores and larger supermarkets.

Ingredients
4 cups (500 g) confectioners' sugar
1 egg white or equivalent dried egg white (meringue powder) reconstituted
2 tbsp (30 ml) liquid glucose (corn syrup)

1 Sift the sugar into a large bowl and make a well in the center.

2 Pour the egg white and glucose into the well and stir it in. Use your hands or the bread kneading attachment on your mixer to knead the fondant together. Knead until it becomes silky and smooth.

3 Double wrap the fondant in two plastic food bags to prevent it from drying out. It can be used immediately. It does not have to be refrigerated but should be used within a week.

Marshmallow fondant

If you have a dough hook attachment on your mixer it will make kneading this paste much easier. However, it is still possible to make by hand, but it will take a lot of kneading. Buy more marshmallows than the recipe requires if you have children—they may nab them!

Marshmallow fondant should be fine to use in temperatures up to 75°F (24°C). Always keep cakes out of direct sunlight, boxed up if possible, and in a cool cupboard.

Ingredients
8 oz (225 g) white mini marshmallows
1–3 tbsp (15–45 ml) cold water
1 lb (450 g) confectioners' sugar (sifted)
2 oz (60 g) solid vegetable shortening in a shallow bowl

1 Place the marshmallows into a large heatproof bowl along with 1 tbsp (15 ml) of water. Microwave for 30 seconds. Stir and microwave for another 30 seconds. Continue in 30-second segments until the marshmallows have dissolved. It should take 1–2 minutes.

2 Tip three-quarters of the sugar on top of the marshmallow mixture and fold it in using a spatula or long metal spoon.

3 Grab a large handful of the vegetable shortening and grease both your hands and your worktop. Tip the mixture out and knead it as you would bread, by pulling and pushing the dough, continually folding it over. Add the rest of the sugar as you go and keep regreasing your hands. By the end you should have used up all the fat and sugar. It could take up to 10 minutes of kneading and it will be messy!

4 When you have created a large dough-like lump of silky fondant—which should stretch if you pull a section off—double wrap it in plastic wrap or a resealable food bag. The fondant will be very soft at first and is at its best if allowed to sit and mature for a few hours before use, ideally overnight.

Using poured fondant

Poured fondant will give you a lovely smooth finish on your cupcakes.

Heat the poured fondant in a glass measuring cup according to the package instructions. Slowly pour the fondant onto your cupcake until it almost reaches the top of the liner. Tap the cupcake on the work surface to remove any air bubbles, then quickly add any decorations, because this fondant sets almost instantly!

FIX IT

67 CRACKING UP?
If the dough gets dry add a little vegetable shortening or a little water—about ½ tbsp (75 ml) at a time. If it gets too wet add sugar. You can add a little vegetable shortening to store-bought fondant if necessary, but use sparingly.

Coloring fondant

Although you can buy colored fondant, it is very easy to color your own. The advantage of this is that you can achieve whatever shade or depth of color you want, rather than being limited by what your local cake decorating store may have in stock.

◀ In the mix
You can achieve a wide variety of colors by mixing colored fondant using the principles you'd use for paint.

Mixing quantities

Make sure you color enough fondant for your project, because it is difficult to match the color when you run out and have to make more.

What type of food coloring?

When coloring fondant it is best to use food color pastes or gels rather than liquids. Pastes and gels are thicker than liquid colors and extremely concentrated, so you shouldn't need to use as much and they are less likely to alter the consistency of the fondant. If you only have liquid colors then keep their use to a minimum, and if the fondant does start to get too wet, knead some extra confectioners' sugar back in.

Another option is to knead lumps of different-colored fondant together—black and white to make gray or yellow and red to make orange.

Some deep colors, such as red and black, can use a lot of color and take a lot of effort to achieve, so it might be worth buying these shades ready colored.

How to get flat matte color

Follow this step-by-step demonstration to discover the essential techniques for coloring fondant. Apply the steps using your chosen color.

1 Lightly dust your work surface with confectioners' sugar to help prevent the fondant from sticking. Knead the fondant until it is warm and pliable.

2 Apply dabs of food color paste to the kneaded fondant. To prevent your pot of food color becoming contaminated, use a fresh toothpick, then throw it away afterward.

3 Begin to knead the color into the fondant. If you are worried about staining, wear disposable food gloves.

4 The fondant will look streaky at first. Continue kneading until it is entirely mixed and you have a flat matte color.

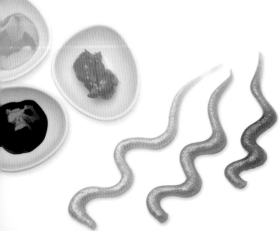

71

Mixing skin tones

It is possible to buy ready-colored fondant in various skin tones. These should be easily available either in your nearest cake-decorating equipment store or via an online store.

Alternatively, you can color your own fondant using food color pastes or gels. There are various shades of food color paste that you can buy to achieve different skin tones. Paprika or chestnut are two of the most commonly used colors to make a pinkish skin tone. You will only need a tiny dash of color. For darker shades, use dark brown or more chestnut food color paste.

You can also make flesh tones by kneading together different-colored lumps of fondant.

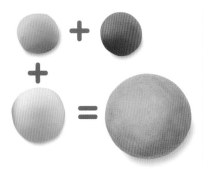

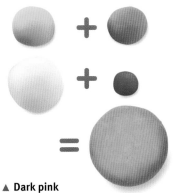

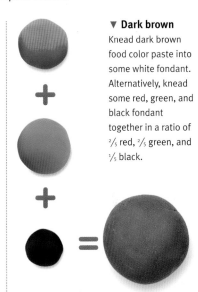

▼ Dark brown
Knead dark brown food color paste into some white fondant. Alternatively, knead some red, green, and black fondant together in a ratio of $2/5$ red, $2/5$ green, and $1/5$ black.

▲ Light pink
Use white fondant and add a tiny dash of "paprika" or "chestnut" food color paste and knead in. Alternatively, knead some white, pink, and yellow fondant together in a ratio of $1/2$ white, $1/4$ yellow, and $1/4$ pink.

▲ Dark pink
Add slightly more "paprika" or "chestnut" food color paste to a lump of white and knead in. Alternatively, knead some white, pink, and yellow fondant together in a ratio of $1/2$ white, $1/4$ yellow, and $1/4$ pink. Then add a little red.

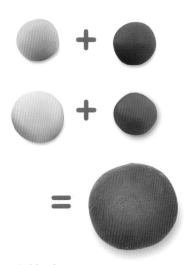

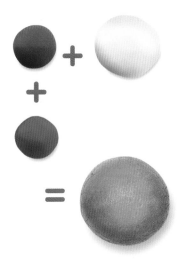

▲ Golden brown
Use white fondant and a dash of food color in a shade called "autumn leaf." Alternatively, knead white, yellow, red, and green fondant together in a ratio of $2/5$ white, $1/5$ yellow, $1/5$ red, and $1/5$ green.

▲ Light brown
Use white fondant and knead in a little "chestnut" food color paste. Alternatively, knead some white, red, and green fondant together in a ratio of $3/5$ white, $1/5$ red, and $1/5$ green.

FIX IT

72 CHANGING THE SHADE
You can always lighten a shade by kneading more white fondant back in, or darken a shade by adding more color.

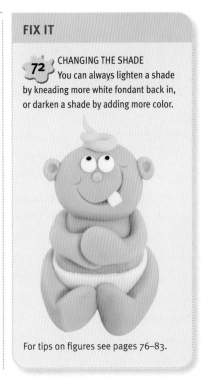

For tips on figures see pages 76–83.

Create a woodgrain effect

This is a useful technique to know about if you ever need to make fondant floorboards—to place around a bed-shaped cake or a chair cake, for example.

1 Roll some white fondant into a thick, chunky sausage shape and apply some streaks of food color paste with a toothpick. You can use just one shade of brown food coloring, or a mixture (dark brown and chestnut, for example).

2 Fold the fondant sausage over onto itself and reroll into a sausage shape.

3 Keep rolling, folding, and rerolling the sausage until you can see the woodgrain effect appearing.

4 Roll the fondant out and apply it to your cake or board.

TRY IT

74 **MARBLING**
Combine a sausage of white fondant with some streaks of food color paste and knead together, but stop when the fondant is at the streaky stage and roll it out. The fondant will have taken on a marbled appearance. This is a useful technique for making a watery effect or for covering a cake that is supposed to look as though it has been made out of marble.

Fondant floorboards

Fondant floorboards are both effective and simple to make. If you want to add a rug, cut out a fondant rectangle, cut a fringe along two opposite ends and place onto your fondant floor.

1 Using a pastry brush, lightly moisten the surface of the cake board with a little water.

2 Begin to roll out the fondant on your work surface then place it onto the board. Continue to roll the fondant up to and over the edges of the board. Trim away any excess fondant.

3 Using a ruler, press lines into the fondant to form the "boards."

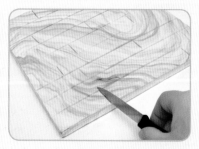

4 Using the back of a small knife, press a few lines across a few of the boards to give the impression of shorter boards.

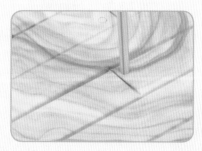

5 Using a drinking straw, press two circles on either side of the shorter board lines. These will look like nail heads in the boards. Place your decorated cake on top.

Spots, stripes, and other delights

If your cake design requires a large area of pattern, you can craft colored effects and patterns on fondant using more fondant. This type of effect is useful if you're creating a cake in the shape of a wrapped parcel, or if you just want an abstract covering for a birthday cake.

Spots

1 Make 10–15 small ⅛ oz (5 g) fondant balls in the colors of your choice and place to one side. Depending upon the size of cake you're covering, you may need fewer or more balls. Lay a sheet of plastic wrap over them to stop them from drying out.
2 Begin to roll out the fondant that you plan to use to cover your cake, but stop before it gets too thin.
3 Place the small fondant balls onto the sheet of fondant and stick them down with light dabs of water.
4 Continue to roll over the sheet of fondant. This will flatten the balls into the icing and creates a pattern.
5 Lay the fondant sheet over your cake, smooth it into place, and trim, then neaten the edges.

Stripes

To make a striped effect follow the same procedure as for the spots, except this time lay long, thin strings of fondant across the fondant base.

Flowers

Follow the spots and stripes process but this time, using a five-petal flower cutter, cut out some thick fondant flower shapes and lightly stick them onto the base fondant. Cut out disks for the flower centers and place one in the middle of each flower. Roll over the whole sheet to flatten it, then place it over your cake.

Parcel cake

This cake is a useful design to have in your repertoire since it can be used for all sorts of occasions. For example, fondant holly and berries would make a striking parcel design for Christmas.

1 Spread some buttercream around the top and sides of a square or rectangular cake. Cover the cake using your patterned fondant.

2 Using the back of a knife, press a "V" shape into two opposite ends of the parcel to represent the folds.

3 Lay two strips of fondant ribbon across the cake and hold in place with either small dabs of buttercream or a little tacky fondant—dip a small fondant ball in water and work it in your fingers until it's sticky. Finish off with a decorative fondant bow (see page 67).

Storing and transporting fondant

Fondant is a fairly hardy and substantial type of cake covering and can last in its airtight package for a long while. Once the package is opened and your cake is decorated it is easy to store as long as you observe a few simple rules.

Storing fondant

Store-bought fondant will arrive sealed in airtight packaging. It will have a "best before" date.

Once the package is open, the fondant has a limited lifespan in which it can be used before it starts to dry out and harden as it comes into contact with air. Once you open the package it is important that any unused fondant is rewrapped tightly in a small resealable food bag. Plastic wrap can be used in an emergency but it will not keep the fondant soft for as long as food bags do. Place the bags into a large airtight plastic container and store in a cool, dark cupboard.

Homemade fondant should be treated in exactly the same way. Neither homemade nor store-bought fondant should be kept in the fridge.

Avoid fading colors

Fondant will fade in bright light—particularly sunlight and even fluorescent light. To prevent this from happening, place any fondant that is being stored in an airtight plastic container and then into a cupboard.

Keep finished cakes or fondant models in a cardboard cake box with a lid. This will not only protect your work from light damage, it will also protect it from dust and insects.

► Pretty presentation

There is a whole host of wonderful ways to present friends and family with your cupcake creations.

Storing models

If you are making 50 fondant teddy bears to put on top of cupcakes for a children's party you may well need to think about making them in advance, a few at a time. This is completely possible. As mentioned above, keep them in a cardboard cake box until required. Do not place finished fondant models in an airtight plastic container or pan because they will begin to sweat and start to droop.

Refrigeration

Whether it's an unopened package of fondant, a decorated fondant cake, or a simple fondant model, fondant should never be kept in the fridge because the dampness inside the fridge will cause the fondant to become too moist.

Freezing

You cannot freeze fondant models or fondant-covered cakes. If you want to get ahead by freezing a cake, you can bake, cool, slice, and fill a cake with buttercream and freeze it at this stage, tightly wrapped in plastic wrap. When you need it, let it defrost overnight and then coat the outside with buttercream and cover with your fondant.

◄ Boxed up

A cake box is ideal for storing and transporting models. If you can't get hold of a cake box you could use a cardboard box and cover it with wrapping paper. Cover up a cellophane window if storing for a long time to avoid light damage.

Transporting fondant

The best method by far for both storing and transporting a fondant-covered cake is to use a cardboard cake box. Purpose-built boxes are available in many sizes, all designed to fit and hold a cake snugly in place on a board. They usually comprise two parts, a base and a lid, and are available in either thin or thick cardboard, the latter being for a cake that has to travel long distances. Boxes are readily available online or from any cake-decorating store.

Transporting tall cakes

If you are transporting a cake that is taller than the height of the box, you will have to extend the height of its sides. Measure the height of the cake and add about 1 in (2.5 cm) to that measurement. Use a sheet of cardstock or a cereal box and cut out four sections that you can staple or tape to the sides of the box to extend its height to the required measurement. Assemble the now taller box and put the lid on top.

FIX IT

 ADAPT THE CAKE BOX
If the box is too big for your cake or the cake has decorations that overhang the edges of the cake board, you will need to use a nonslip mat to hold the cake in place. This is available at cake craft stores or on the Internet, and is a thin rubber mat that you can cut to size. Place a rectangle in the base of the box and the cake on its board on the top, and the cake will stay still in the box.

Moving cupcakes

Once upon a time, cupcakes were unlovingly crammed into a normal cake box or even a flat cardboard vegetable box from the supermarket. But the meteoric rise in popularity of cupcakes over the past few years has led to the cupcake having many modes of transport specially designed for it. These range from plain, flat boxes and boxes with partitions to special clear plastic carriers, which will transport your creations safely to their destination. Any of these methods are fine; the only note of caution is, if you are using the plastic cake carriers to carry cakes with fondant decorations, then try not to leave your cakes sealed inside for too long, because fondant may start to droop and sweat in airtight conditions.

Keeping cake pops intact

How do you transport 50 swaying cake pops on lollipop sticks? The cheap and easy answer is to wedge a thick section of polystyrene into a box or boxes and poke the lollipop sticks into that. The pops can then be displayed in small jars or glasses at the party. However, you can buy acrylic and cardboard cake pop holders online or from cake-decoration stores, which are fancy enough to transport the pops safely and to appear at the party!

Covering cake with fondant

No matter how many fantastic models and decorations you plan to adorn your cake with, the cake itself will still need to be covered. Fondant is an ideal covering because it is easy to use and will seal in the cake, keeping it fresher for slightly longer.

Quantities for cake coverings

The table opposite will give you an idea of how much fondant you need for each size of cake. You can add to or reduce the amounts depending upon how thick or thin you like your cake coverings to be. You can also use these amounts for covering cakes using marzipan.

Covering round cakes

A round cake is probably the easiest shape to cover. If you are using a pound cake it should be leveled, split, filled with buttercream, and be sitting on a cake board ready for covering. It should also have a thin coating of jam or buttercream over the top and sides. This will glue the fondant to the sides of the cake.

If you are covering a fruitcake it should be covered with a layer of marzipan first to stop the oils from the cake seeping through the fondant. Use a pastry brush to lightly dampen the marzipan with some cooled boiled water. This will make it sticky and allow it to hold the fondant in place.

1 Lightly dust your work surface with confectioners' sugar and knead the fondant until it is soft and pliable. For fondant quantities see the chart opposite.

2 Roll the fondant out using a rolling pin. Fondant is easier to use if it's not rolled too thinly, so don't roll it out to any less than ⅓ in (7 mm). To ensure that it's the same thickness all the way through you can lay a pair of cake spacers on either side of the fondant and roll over them as you roll out the icing.

3 Lift the fondant and place it over the top of the cake. You can do this by sliding your hands flat, palms uppermost, under the fondant and lifting and placing it over the cake. Alternatively, you can roll the fondant loosely around the rolling pin and unroll it over the top of the cake.

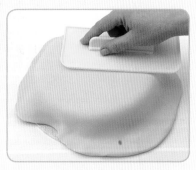

4 Smooth the icing into position over the top of the cake. You can use your hands to do this, but a cake smoother will give you a better finish. Use it to smooth over the top and sides of the cake.

QUANTITY GUIDE FOR FONDANT AND MARZIPAN

SQUARE PAN		6 in (15 cm)	7 in (18 cm)	8 in (20 cm)	9 in (23 cm)	10 in (25 cm)	11 in (28 cm)	12 in (30 cm)
ROUND PAN	6 in (15 cm)	7 in (18 cm)	8 in (20 cm)	9 in (23 cm)	10 in (25 cm)	11 in (28 cm)	12 in (30 cm)	
FONDANT OR MARZIPAN	1 lb 2 oz (500 g)	1 lb 5 oz (650 g)	1 lb 12 oz (800 g)	2 lb (900 g)	2 lb 8 oz (1.1 kg)	3 lb (1.4 kg)	3 lb 8 oz (1.6 kg)	4 lb (1.8 kg)

5 Smooth the icing down the sides of the cake to the board. The icing may fan out a little around the base. Simply lift and press it into place. Again, run around the sides with a cake smoother if you have one.

6 To finish, cut away and keep the excess fondant from around the base of the cake.

85

Covering square cakes

The technique for covering a square cake is virtually the same as for a round cake, although you do need to be a little more careful with the corners. Allow the fondant to fall over the corners and gently smooth it into place. Smooth the top first to try and prevent air getting trapped, then carefully ease it over and down the sides. Fondant will produce a gentle rounded effect on edges and corners.

FIX IT

86 REMOVING AIR BUBBLES
If an air bubble gets trapped under the fondant, take a clean dressmaker's pin and, holding it at an angle, gently prick the air bubble. Carefully press the fondant back into position afterward.

87

Covering large cakes

If you need to cover a large cake with fondant you may find it helpful to support the roll of fondant as you do so. The best way to do this is to slide a large cake board under the rolled out fondant, then slide it over the cake.

▼ Covering dummy cakes

To cover a polysterene dummy, moisten it with water and cover with fondant as you would for a real cake.

88

Covering letter- and number-shaped cakes

Many numbers and letters can be covered at one time, like a square or round cake, but others, such as "3" or "E" can be more difficult. With these characters it's better to cover them in two parts: top first and then the sides.

1 Level and slice the cake into layers as usual and place the base layer on the cake board.

2 Spread your filling over the base layer and assemble the cake. Spread a coating of buttercream or jam around the top and sides of the assembled cake.

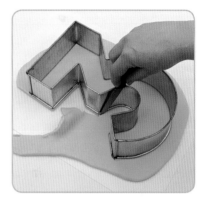

3 Knead and roll out the fondant. Using the baking pan as a template, cut out the shape of the number or letter and place it on top of the cake. Cut away any excess.

4 Measure the height of the cake and paint a line of water along the vertical edge of the fondant you have just laid on top of the cake.

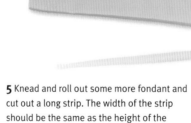

5 Knead and roll out some more fondant and cut out a long strip. The width of the strip should be the same as the height of the cake. Roll it up like a loose bandage.

6 Holding the "bandage" vertically, unwind it around the cake. You can hide the seam around the top edge of the cake either by crimping around the edges with a crimping tool, piping a line of piping, or simply by sticking a line of sweets along the edge.

FIX IT

89 FILLING THE CRACKS

If you get slight cracking on the edges of the cake it probably means that the fondant was not fresh enough and had begun to dry out. If you have covered your cake with white fondant you may find that gently rubbing a little confectioners' sugar into the cracks with your fingertip will suffice. If you are still not happy, you could place a decoration over the top or crimp around the edges of the cake (see page 71).

Measuring with your rolling pin

You can use your rolling pin as a measuring device to ensure that you have rolled out enough icing. Hold the rolling pin over the top of the cake and measure its width against the rolling pin. Place a finger at this point and add about another 5 in (12 cm) to that measurement to take into account the sides of the cake. Now move your finger along the rolling pin to that point. Hold the rolling pin over the rolled out fondant to see if it's large enough. Fondant will stretch, so you do have some leeway.

Soften the fondant

You can place the fondant in the microwave for 15 seconds on the highest setting to soften it. Don't heat for too long, otherwise the fondant will melt and burn.

Double covering

Double covering, as its name implies, means covering a cake twice, either with marzipan followed by fondant, or with two coats of fondant. Although by no means essential, it might be worth considering doing this on an important pound cake, such as a wedding cake, where the best possible finish is required. Fruitcake is always covered twice, first with marzipan and then with fondant or royal icing.

Keep your buttercream fresh

To prevent the buttercream on the cake from drying out while you roll out the fondant, place a sheet of plastic wrap over it and remove it just before covering the cake.

TRY IT

91 USING AN EDGER
A tool called an edger was developed especially for covering the cake and its board at one time. Its flat base smoothes the fondant on the board, while its flat side smoothes the fondant on the sides of the cake, all in one motion.

▶ **Beautiful edges**
If, when covering your cake, your fondant seams are less than perfect you can disguise them with some buttercream piping. This can be particularly useful for unusually-shaped cakes that are tricky to cover neatly.

Covering boards

There are various ways to cover a board around a cake, and different techniques suit different designs. However, it is not absolutely necessary, and if you are new to the craft, or simply very pushed for time, you could always take advantage of a pretty pre-decorated cake board instead!

95

Covering the entire board

This is the easiest way to cover a board. Your decorated cake can then be placed on top.

TRY IT

96 DECORATING THE CAKE BOARD
Your board doesn't have to be plain; you could add some pretty detail by pressing a cutter or the end of a drinking straw into the still-soft fondant to create a pattern.

GUIDELINE AMOUNTS OF FONDANT FOR COVERING CAKE BOARDS

		6 in (15 cm)	7 in (18 cm)	8 in (20 cm)	9 in (23 cm)	10 in (25 cm)	11 in (28 cm)	12 in (30 cm)
SQUARE PAN		6 in (15 cm)	7 in (18 cm)	8 in (20 cm)	9 in (23 cm)	10 in (25 cm)	11 in (28 cm)	12 in (30 cm)
ROUND PAN	6 in (15 cm)	7 in (18 cm)	8 in (20 cm)	9 in (23 cm)	10 in (25 cm)	11 in (28 cm)	12 in (30 cm)	
FONDANT	10 oz (300 g)	11 oz (325 g)	15 oz (420 g)	1 lb 4 oz (550 g)	1 lb 7 oz (650 g)	1 lb 12 oz (800 g)	2 lb 2 oz (1 kg)	2 lb 12 oz (1.2 kg)

1 Using a pastry brush and water, lightly dampen the surface of the board.

2 Knead and begin to roll out the fondant, then place it onto the middle of the board.

3 Continue to roll the fondant up to and over the edges of the board.

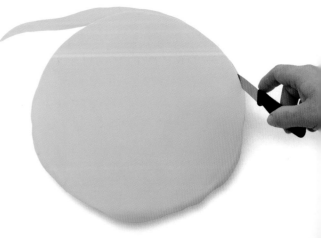

4 Trim away the excess and neaten the edges. Put the board to one side until needed again.

97

The bandage method

As its name implies, this technique involves winding the fondant like a bandage and unwinding it around the cake on the board. It will only work for a round or curved cake.

3 Slice a little fondant away from one long side of the strip to make one neat edge.

1 With your cake already covered and in situ on the board, lightly dampen the exposed cake board with a little water. Measure the circumference of the cake and the width of the exposed board.

2 Knead and roll out some fondant—you'll need to cut a strip slightly wider than the width of the exposed board and as long as the circumference of the cake. Slide a palette knife under the strip to ensure that it's not stuck to your work surface.

4 Carefully roll the fondant up as though it were a bandage.

5 With the neat edge against the side of the cake, unwind the strip around the cake on the board.

6 Trim and neaten the seam and the edges of the board.

98

Covering the cake and board together

To do this you will need to use more fondant than you usually would to allow for covering the board as well. Before you start, coat the outside of the cake with jam or buttercream and lightly moisten the exposed cake board with a little water. You will need a minimum of 8 oz (250 g) of extra fondant to allow for covering the board as well.

1 Knead and roll out the fondant and place it over the top of the cake allowing the fondant to cover the board as well. Press it into place.

2 Smooth the top and sides with an edger and trim away the excess fondant from around the board.

99

Covering a board in sections

Covering a board with fondant around a straight-edged cake, such as a square or rectangle, takes a little more time than for a round cake and is a little trickier, but is well worth mastering.

1 Moisten the exposed cake board around the base of the cake with a little water. Measure the width of the exposed board and also the length of the board.

2 Roll out some fondant thinly. The amount will vary depending upon how much board you have to cover. It is generally in the region of 8 oz–1 lb 2 oz (250 g–500 g). Cut out four wide strips and lay one on each section of the board.

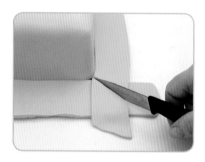

3 Using a sharp knife cut a diagonal line from one corner of the board to the diagonally corresponding corner of the cake.

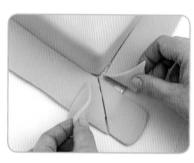

4 Carefully remove the two excess sections of fondant. You should now be left with a neat seam. Repeat on the other three corners of the board.

5 Trim away the excess fondant from around the edges and smooth with a smoother.

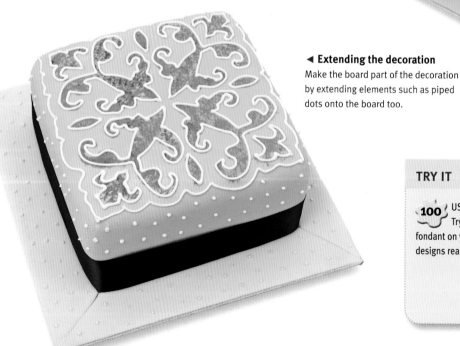

◄ **Extending the decoration**
Make the board part of the decoration by extending elements such as piped dots onto the board too.

TRY IT

100 USE A CONTRASTING COLOR
Try using a contrasting color of fondant on your board to make your designs really stand out.

101
Create the look of fabric

This technique involves rolling out the fondant and then allowing it to fall into folds on the board around the cake to resemble fabric.

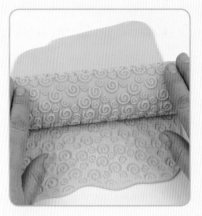

1 The covered cake should be in position on the cake board. Lightly paint a little water around the exposed cake board using a soft pastry brush.

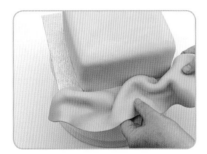

2 Roll out the fondant to a thickness of about ¼ in (5 mm). Lift and place a section of fondant onto the board, allowing it to drape and fall into soft folds as you go.

3 Continue all around the cake until the board is covered. Then cut away any excess fondant that is hanging over the edges of the board to make it neat and tidy.

104
Adding texture

As its name suggests, a textured rolling pin adds texture to fondant. You use it just like a normal rolling pin, and as it rolls it imprints a texture or pattern onto the fondant. Textured rolling pins are available in a variety of patterns.

TRY IT

102   CREATING TEXTURED
FABRIC FONDANT

Try combining the fabric effect with a textured rolling pin; this combination can make your fabric effect look even more realistic.

103
Pressed effects

You can press cutters, letters, and even the back of your knife into the cake board to add extra visual interest to your cake and enhance your overall design.

Painting and drawing on fondant

Painting and drawing may not be the first method of decoration that you think of when you design a cake, but it does offer a lot of interesting effects and options.

Painting pictures

If possible, allow the covered cake to harden overnight before painting. You will be less likely to dent the surface.

1 Gently brush the top of the cake with a soft brush to remove any confectioners' sugar.

2 Lightly paint the outline of your shape onto the cake using either watered-down food coloring or a food color pen.

▲ **Standing out**
This large pattern will photograph well, which is important for a special event such as a wedding.

Transferring designs

If you don't want to freehand paint your design straight onto your cake, you could transfer it instead. First, draw or trace your image onto greaseproof paper. Then place it on your cake in the desired position and use a scriber to prick your design through on to the cake. You can then go over the work with food coloring or a food color pen.

3 Fill in the outline with food coloring.

4 Alternatively, you could use cocoa powder as your paint. To do this just mix a little melted vegetable shortening with the cocoa powder and get painting.

FIX IT

107 REMOVING A MISTAKE
If you make a mistake, dab it with a soft brush and clean water, wipe away the color with a soft clean cloth, and wait for the area to dry before repainting.

 108

Painted fondant shapes

This is an easy way to create a pattern on big cakes and cupcakes. It is also a way to feature lots of colors without having to mix different batches of fondant colors for each one.

1 Using the cutter of your choice, cut out some fondant shapes. They need to be at least ¼ in (5 mm) thick.

2 Allow the shapes to harden, then paint the tops with food coloring and allow to dry.

3 If you're decorating a large cake, arrange and stick the shapes on top of your cake with dabs of water or royal icing. If you're decorating cupcakes, simply place them on top of the buttercream.

 109

Stenciling on fondant

Stenciling onto cakes has become very popular recently, and there are many attractive stencils available. It's worth noting that stencils need not just be used with food coloring, you can stencil using confectioners' sugar, cocoa powder, royal icing, and edible food dusts as well.

1 Place the stencil in position on your cake.

2 Dab a thick paintbrush into some watered-down food coloring and blot the excess on some paper towel. Gently dab the brush over the stencil.

TRY IT

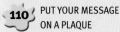 **110** PUT YOUR MESSAGE ON A PLAQUE

If you're nervous about painting or drawing a picture or message directly onto the cake, cut out a fondant plaque or strip of fondant and paint or draw your message onto the plaque or banner (see pages 72–75 for tips on writing on fondant). If you go wrong you can just try again on another plaque. Once you are happy with your design you can attach it to your cake with a dab of water.

3 Carefully remove the stencil to reveal the pattern.

111

Stenciling draped fondant

Draping fondant is a great way to introduce strong colors like black onto your cake without the fear of making a mistake, since the piece can easily be removed if you are not happy with it. With a drape it is best to go for a stencil with a random pattern rather than a specific image—it will be laid onto your cake much like fabric and will crease, so parts of the image could be lost, thus ruining the desired effect.

1 Roll out some fondant mixed with gum tragacanth onto a work surface lightly dusted with confectioners' sugar to approximately ⅛ in (3 mm) thick. Don't roll it any thinner because it will rip when you lift it. Make sure you use enough confectioners' sugar to ensure that the fondant does not stick to the work surface.

2 Cut out your drape using a sharp knife. Either measure the side of your cake with a tape measure or, if you are confident, lift your piece of fondant up to the side of your cake to check for sizing.

3 Place the stencil on the fondant. Load one side of a spatula with buttercream or royal icing and draw it over the stencil.

4 Paint the area of the cake where the drape is going with royal icing, then very carefully lift your drape onto the cake and position it, trying where possible to avoid touching the surface of the drape and disturbing the stenciled pattern. Let it dry completely once it is in position.

▲ **Draped fondant**
A draped piece of fondant can provide a splash of drama to an otherwise simply decorated cake.

112

Designing your own stencil

Draw your design onto cardstock and carefully cut it out using a craft knife. Use books or the Internet for inspiration. Place the stencil on your cake and carefully sponge or use a paintbrush to dab color on through the cutout sections.

113

Sponging with food coloring

For a quick cake decorating idea, dip a clean sponge into a little watered-down food coloring. Blot it onto some paper towel to remove the excess liquid (if it's too wet, the color will run down the sides of the cake) and gently press onto the cake.

Stenciling on cookies

Stenciling on a fondant disk is a stylish way to bring a bit of glamor to a plain and uninspiring cookie.

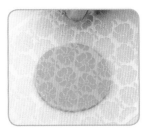

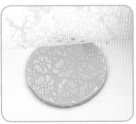

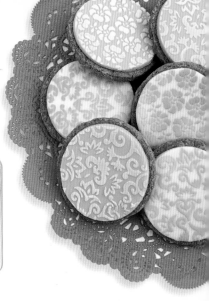

1 Cut out a fondant disk and place the stencil on top of it.

2 Load up one side of your spatula with slightly thinned royal icing and, holding it at an angle, draw it over the stencil across the top of the fondant.

3 Gently raise the stencil and allow it to dry. Stick it on top of the cookie with a little water or a dab of royal icing.

▲ **Time-saving stenciling**
If you have a big stencil you may find it better to roll out a large lump of fondant, stencil a bigger area and cut out as many disks as you can at the same time.

Create a tartan effect

For this technique you will need a small artist's roller with a sponge attachment. If you are using more than one color it is best to wait for the first color to dry before applying the second.

1 Place some watered-down food coloring into a saucer and run the roller through it.

2 Run the roller over some paper towel to remove the excess liquid, then roll it over the cake. Roll over the fondant both horizontally and vertically, then allow to dry.

Sponging with royal icing

Mix up some royal icing to a medium-thin consistency and use a piece of sea sponge to apply the icing to the fondant. Twist your wrist back and forth as you dab. It's fun to use two colors of royal icing, and white works particularly well for winter cakes.

3 Clean the roller or add a different width of sponge and repeat with the second color. Allow to dry.

4 To finish, draw lines horizontally and vertically across the fondant using a thin paintbrush or a food color pen.

Fondant frills and fancies

A cake decorated with draping and frilling around its sides is always impressive and intriguing people. Although the decoration looks intricate, fondant makes these effects fairly easy to create.

 117

Making drapes

The most important thing about draping a cake is trying to make all the drapes equal so that the cake looks balanced. The base cake should be covered with fondant and ideally have been left overnight for the fondant to harden before you start.

▲ Combining looks
Using a mixture of drapes, bows, and piping will create an interesting and elegant cake.

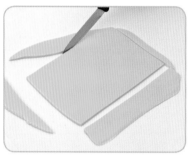

1 Make a small mark on the edge of the cake with a food color pen or toothpick. Make a corresponding mark directly opposite it. Depending on how many drapes you want to use, make another two or three marks between the two original marks and another two or three opposite them. The marks should be equally spaced apart.

2 Measure the distance between two of the marks, thinly roll out a little fondant and cut out a rectangle. The rectangle should be slightly longer than the gap between the marks and its width should match the height of the cake.

3 Concertina the rectangle into two or three folds.

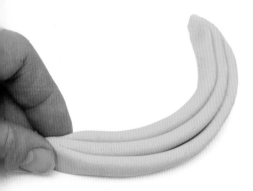

5 Using a little water, stick the drape onto the cake between two of the marks. Repeat and continue all around the cake, adding drapes between the marks. You can hide the seams with fondant bows or other decorations.

4 Pinch the ends and bend the drape into a "U" shape.

Making frills

Fondant can be used to make delicate frills around the sides of your cake. Although not essential, a cutter called a Garrett frill cutter is useful for making these elaborate flounces.

1 Divide your cake into sections as shown opposite. Dust your work surface with confectioners' sugar to stop the fondant from sticking. Thinly roll out a little fondant and cut out a disk using the Garrett frill cutter.

2 Take a toothpick and gently roll it backward and forward over the patterned edge. A frill should start to appear. Gradually move all the way along the edge.

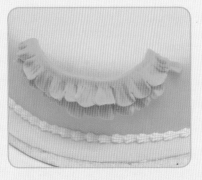

3 Paint a light line of water in a "U" shape on the cake. Cut open the frilled circle and carefully lift and stick the frill in place. Repeat around the cake.

4 Add a second line of frills above the first if you wish.

5 If it looks a bit untidy you can hide the edge of the frill with a line of piping or crimping. If you aren't serving your frilled cake immediately, make sure you store it in a box away from any dampness, otherwise the frills will quickly lose their perkiness.

TRY IT

119 VARY THE FRILLS
- Frills can go up or down! Stick the frills the other way around for a different effect.
- Frill cutters also come with straight edges, so you can make a line of frilling around your cake instead of a curve.
- Make a frilled plaque for piping a message by cutting out a fondant disk with your frill cutter and frilling around the edges.

Improvising a cutter

Even if you don't own a Garrett frill cutter you can still achieve a similar frilled effect using a jam tart cutter.

121

Making molded drapes

It is now possible to buy molds for drapes, which makes creating identical drapes easy.

1 Dust the inside of the mold with confectioners' sugar, or rub a little white vegetable shortening inside to aid the release of the drape.

2 Roll out a strip of fondant and press it into the mold.

3 Slice the excess off the back of the mold using a sharp knife so that the drape will sit flush against the side of the cake when you turn it out.

4 Gently push the mold from behind and pull the drape out of the mold.

5 Stick the drape against the side of the cake with a little water. Repeat all the way around the cake.

122 HALLOWEEN HORRORS
Draw a simple ghost shape onto a sheet of wafer paper with a black food color pen. Cut the ghost out and stand it in orange buttercream on top of a green cupcake. Try out any of the templates below to add some variety to your Halloween treats.

123

Edible wafer decorations

Edible wafer paper, also known as rice paper, is one of the most useful things to have in your decorating store cupboard. It can be used for so many things—fairy wings, butterflies, messages, and because it's edible it can be left safely on the cake. It's available in different colors too!

Dipped chocolate edible paper
You can make these decorations simply and easily. Just cut your shape out of the paper, then dip one side into some melted chocolate and leave to cool. You can attach them to your cake with a dab of buttercream.

Edible messages and pictures
Create a message or drawing on a piece of wafer paper with a food safe pen and place onto the cake.

124

Wafer preparation

Get organized by making your wafer paper designs well in advance of the party. Keep them in a box until required.

125 WAFER CURLS
Cut some thin strips out of colored wafer paper and wind them around a pencil. Place the curls onto your cake.

▼ **Terrifying templates**
Here are some templates for horrid wafer designs for your Halloween celebrations.

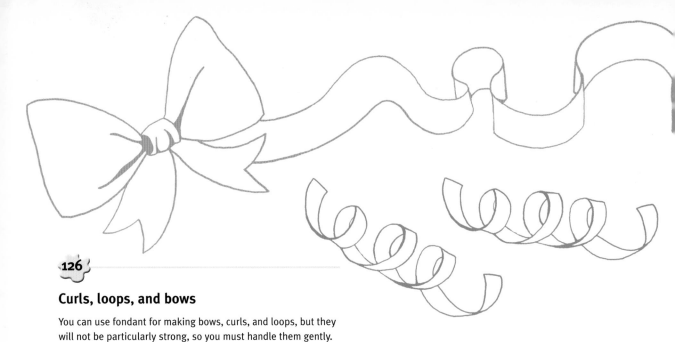

Curls, loops, and bows

You can use fondant for making bows, curls, and loops, but they will not be particularly strong, so you must handle them gently.

Making curls

Curls are very fragile, so handle them carefully when lifting and arranging them onto the cake. The smaller the curls the stronger they will be.

Making loops

As with curls, loops are very delicate and need to be handled with care to prevent breakages.

1 Dust your work surface with a little confectioners' sugar and thinly roll out 8 oz (250 g) of fondant. You will need to allow 1 oz (30 g) per loop. Cut out a number of rectangles about 3 in x 1 in (8 cm x 2.5 cm) in size. They can be larger or smaller depending on how big or small you want your loops to be. Cut a triangle into each end.

2 Roll each strip around a rolling pin and stick the ends together with a light dab of water. The smaller the loop the stronger it will be.

1 Use 1 oz (30 g) of fondant per curl and roll it out no thinner than ⅛ in (3 mm). Cut out a flat strip of 6 in x ½ in (15 cm x 1.5 cm). Carefully wind the strip around a small rolling stick, wooden spoon handle, or something similar and allow the fondant to harden.

2 When the outside has firmed up, carefully remove the internal support and let the inside of the curl harden. Gently lift and place the curls onto the cake and secure them with a light dab of water or a couple of dots of royal icing.

3 Leave to dry somewhere warm. Remove the central support when the outside is hard enough and allow the insides of the loops to harden. Arrange and stick onto the cake with light dabs of water or dots of royal icing.

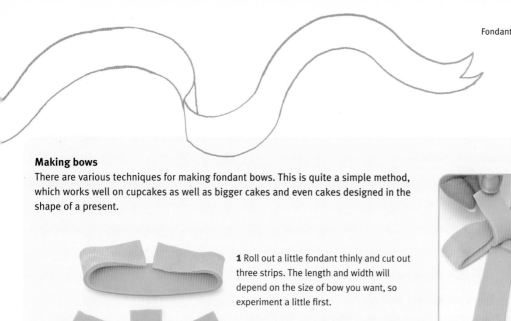

Making bows

There are various techniques for making fondant bows. This is quite a simple method, which works well on cupcakes as well as bigger cakes and even cakes designed in the shape of a present.

1 Roll out a little fondant thinly and cut out three strips. The length and width will depend on the size of bow you want, so experiment a little first.

2 Cut one strip in half and cut a triangle into each end—these will form the tails of the bow. Place them next to each other and tweak them into position.

3 Roll the second strip into a circle, then pinch the center.

4 Cut the last strip in half and discard one half. Stick the second half around the middle of the bow with a little water.

5 Stick the center of the bow onto the bow tails and place in position on your cake.

127

Do the twist

This is a very quick way to decorate the base or the top edge of a cake. Your cake should be covered with fondant or buttercream and be in position on the cake board before you start.

1 Measure the circumference of the cake and roll a ball of fondant into a long string to about the same length. Roll over the string with a rolling pin to flatten it and cut out a long thin strip.

2 Lift and twist the strip. Repeat until you have a long length of twisted fondant.

3 Paint a light line of water around the top edge of the cake or around the board, depending on where you wish to place the twist.

4 Gently lay the twisted strip into position and neaten the seam.

▼ Let's party

Loops, bows, and spirals all together make a fun and versatile party cake. The loops also work well on parcel cakes.

Molds, cutters, and crimpers

There are thousands of molds, cutters, and crimpers available for the cake decorator to choose from. From cheeky faces and angelic babies to ornate bows and beautiful butterflies. If you're at all nervous about freehand modeling there will be a mold somewhere that can help you!

Embossing on fondant

Embossing means "raised design," and there are various ways to create an embossed pattern in fondant. It can be used to decorate the sides of a cake or the edge of a coated cake board. Create designs using something as simple as a plastic doily or piping tips, or achieve more interesting results using leather punches, buttons, or plastic embossers from specialty cake decorating stores.

TRY IT

129 TEXTURED CUPCAKE DECORATIONS
Textured rolling pins can also be used to create an easy embossed pattern for stylish cupcakes.

Roll over a sheet of fondant with a textured rolling pin and, using your chosen cutter, cut out disks to place on top of each one of your cupcakes. To help them stick, dab some apricot jam or buttercream over the top of your cupcakes.

1 While the fondant is still soft, quickly press the embosser into it. Be firm and confident in your application—do not jiggle the embosser or try to emboss twice, since this will be difficult to color later.

2 Quickly work through the varying sizes of embossers to create a varied and interesting design.

3 You can use plain piping tips in varying sizes to create a freestyle "bubble" effect to soften the edges of the design.

4 If you want to color your embossing, a good way to do so is to use a flat dusting brush and a mixture of edible dusting powders to "blush" each motif.

5 You can add an outline and finer detail to the the embossed pattern using a fine paintbrush and some powder, diluted with clear alcohol.

6 Use a decorative button, leather punch, or an embosser to create a pretty decorative edge to a coated cake board.

Face molds on cupcakes

Strictly speaking fondant is not the best type of modeling icing to use in delicate figure molds, because it does not have the strength and plasticity of other types of modeling icing such as flowerpaste or gumpaste. However, used with care on simple, chunky molds you should be able to produce some cheeky little people!

1 Dust the inside of the mold with a little confectioners' sugar.

2 Press some flesh-colored fondant into the mold.

3 Slice the excess fondant away from the back of the mold with a sharp knife. Gently ease the face out of the mold and allow it to dry.

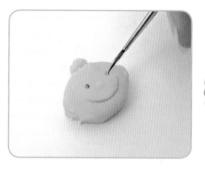

4 Paint features onto the molded face by using food coloring and place the face onto your cupcake.

▲ **All smiles**
If you don't have a mold, you could create your own fondant face see pages 79–83.

Making your own mold

Though you can buy a huge variety of ready-made molds, you may decide that you want to make your own. Molds can be taken from a whole host of materials including fresh petals, pendants, buttons, and shells. It is vital that you use only mold-making mediums that are suitable for use with food items.

1 There are various types of silicone putty available for making molds. The kind shown here is fairly simple to use. It is important to work on a nonstick board since these materials will stick to anything. Measure equal amounts of each compound using a measuring spoon.

2 Mix the two compounds together thoroughly. One compound is a catalyst and once mixed you will have between 10–20 minutes working time before the mixed medium sets—which often depends upon the weather at the time.

3 Flatten the silicone putty against the board and press the original into the compound. (Here, a seahorse brooch was used.) Leave the putty for 10–20 minutes to set, then remove the original. You now have a mold of your original object.

132

All cut up

There are many cutters available to choose from and many can double up as cutters for cookies as well as sugarcraft designs. Cutters are available in plastic and metal. Although more expensive, a metal cutter will usually produce a sharper, neater cut.

▲ Flower cutter
◀ Blossom plunge cutters

Fondant inlays

This is an easy way to create a pattern on a cake. Use the same cutter for creating the inlays as you use for making the cutouts.

1 Cover your cake with fondant as usual then, using a cutter, press it into the icing going right through the fondant until you just touch the cake beneath. Remove the cutout shapes.

2 Roll out some fondant in a contrasting color. Try to make it the same thickness as the cutout pieces and cut out the required number of shapes to fill the spaces on the cake.

3 Place a cutout fondant shapes into each space on the cake.

◀ Heart cutter

TRY IT

133 COVERED COOKIES
Use your cutter to cut out your cookie shapes and bake them. Once cooled, use the same cookie cutter to cut out fondant shapes to decorate the cookies. Use a little apricot jam or buttercream on the back of the fondant to stick the fondant shapes to your cookies.

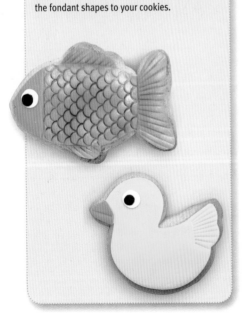

134

Crimping

A crimping tool is incredibly effective for use with fondant or marzipan. A bit like a pair of miniature tongs with decorative ends, crimping tools are used to pinch patterns around the edges of cakes and boards. Crimpers will only work on soft fondant or marzipan, so they are normally used as soon as the cake has been covered and the fondant smoothed, with its base trimmed and in position on its board.

135

Clean crimping

To ensure you achieve clearly defined crimps use a little stiff brush to clean off the dried fondant from the crimper as you are crimping.

▼ **Crimping your style**
Crimpers come in a variety of styles, and each will create a different pattern.

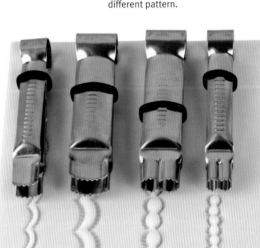

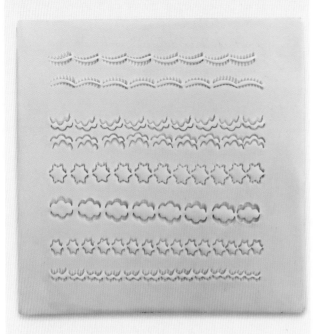

139

Crimping the base of a cake

Position the cake on the board and paint a light line of water around the base of the cake. Roll out a long, thin fondant string and lay it around the cake. Take your crimpers and crimp along the fondant string.

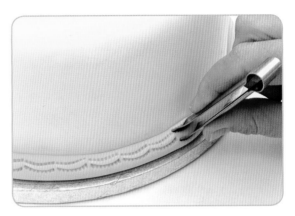

Holding close to the ends of the crimper, pinch a little fondant between them. Gently squeeze together and release. Repeat all the way around the cake. If you're crimping around the top edge of a cake you may find it easier to crimp on the edge of the cake that is farthest away from you, rotating the cake as you go.

136

Crimping around a cake board

Experiment on a spare piece of fondant to see what patterns you can achieve before you work on the board itself. When you are happy with the result and the cake is in position on the fondant-covered board, gently press the crimpers into the soft fondant.

137

Improvised crimpers

If you don't have crimpers you can use other things from around the kitchen to produce a pattern on your board or cake, for example the back of a knife or the edge of a teaspoon.

Another tool that can be used to provide a pattern around the edge of a cake is a pair of kitchen scissors. Make small partial snips around the edge of the cake to produce an interesting fringed effect. Just be careful not to snip right through to the cake beneath.

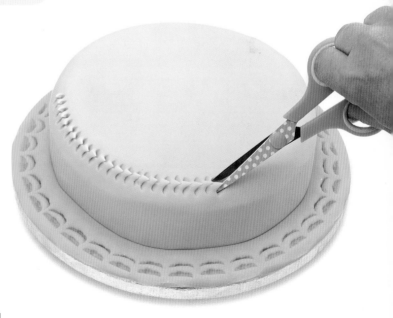

138

Stop the crimper from sticking

Dipping the crimper into a little confectioners' sugar will stop it from sticking and tearing the fondant.

Writing on fondant

For many people, piping a message onto a cake can be daunting. What if it looks awful? What if I make a mistake? What if I underestimate what a long word "congratulations" is? The simple answer is practice. Eventually you will be able to pipe a message with aplomb and confidence, but in the meantime there are various methods that will help you. For piping techniques see pages 114–117.

140

Piping an outline

Clear piping gel and buttercream have many uses, one of which is as a guide for piped messages.

1 Write your message on a piece of baking paper with pencil, then turn the paper over. The message should now be written backward but clearly visible.

2 Pipe over the backward message with a little piping gel or buttercream in a bag fitted with a number 1 piping nozzle.

FIX IT

141 COVERING A MISTAKE
If you make a piped or scribed mistake that marks the fondant surface preventing you from repiping over the area, make a small fondant plaque, place it over the damaged area and pipe your message again.

3 Place the baking paper gel/buttercream side down in position on the cake. Gently trace over the message with a soft paintbrush, then carefully lift the paper.

4 The message should be subtly visible allowing you to pipe neatly over the top.

TRY IT

142 TYPEFACE TEMPLATE
The typeface you decide on for your cake needs to look beautiful, but also be legible. This alphabet has character and is continued over the page along with the numbers.

ABCDEF

Scribing

This is another common method. Write your message on a piece of baking paper first then place it onto the cake and prick the message through using a scriber (a tool a bit like a needle on a stick and available from cake or craft stores). Remove the paper and pipe over the scratched message.

Ideal conditions

To get the best results from lettering transfer techniques such as scribing or the buttercream/gel method, you should allow your fondant-covered cake to firm up overnight. This will give you a great base for writing.

Keeping it straight

It is useful to place a straight piece of heavy paper (about 1 in/2.5 cm wide) on the top of the cake. This will act as a guide and help you to pipe the message in a straight line. It is best to use this with all techniques of writing messages on cakes.

Pressed letters

A more expensive alternative to tracing a typeface is a lettering kit. You slot your message into place and press it into the fondant. The letters leave an imprint behind for you to trace over with your piping nozzle.

This is good for positioning letters, but you are limited to the styles of writing that come with the kit.

GHIJKLMNO

147

Mastering piped messages

When piping a message, ideally, you need to keep an even, sustained flow of icing coming out of the nozzle. You would usually use a plain nozzle number 1, 2, or 3 depending on how thick you want the lettering to be. Practice off the cake first!

1 Squeeze the piping bag and, holding the tip about ½ in (1 cm) above the cake, pipe your letter. If it's a letter with straight edges "A," "E," or "I" etc., pipe one of the straight lines first, allowing the icing to fall and lie on the cake. When your line is long enough, press the tip of the nozzle gently into the icing and stop squeezing. You should be able to lift the nozzle up and the icing should break away from the cake.

2 To pipe a curved section of a letter or number, touch the cake surface with the tip of the nozzle. Squeeze and lift the nozzle, moving your hand so that the icing falls in a curve onto the cake.

3 To finish, press the tip into the end of the curve, release the pressure and the icing should break away. With time, you will develop your own style of piped handwriting and you will eventually be able to pipe directly onto the cake's surface with confidence.

148

Working order

It is usually best to do any writing on the cake early on in your decorating process. It can be very discouraging when you run out of space for your message because you've already placed your fondant flowers or figures on the cake.

149

Penning and painting

If you do not have any royal icing or writing icing to pipe a message on your cake you can always paint a food coloring one or draw one with a food color pen. Again, it is best to do this on a fondant-covered cake that has been allowed to harden overnight.

If you're painting, paint a light outline of your wording first. Weak, watered-down food coloring is good for this. Then paint over the lettering with a darker color to make your message stand out.

If you're using a food color pen, carefully write your message directly onto the fondant.

PQRSTUVWX

150
Plaques and banners

One way to prevent spoiling a cake with a piping or writing error is to put your message onto a fondant banner or plaque. That way, if you make a mistake you can simply replace the banner or plaque without needing to re-cover the whole cake!

Plaques

Cut out a shape for your plaque. You can use a specially designed plaque cutter, a simple jam tart cutter, or a fondant shape. Pipe or write your message on the plaque and stick it onto the cake.

Banners

Make a strip of fondant and cut a small triangle out of either end of the strip. Arrange and stick the banner onto the cake with a few dabs of water. Paint your message on with a little watered-down food coloring, or pipe your message.

151
Letter cutters

For big, bright, and bold messages you could use letter cutters. Alphabet cutters are available in metal and plastic. Roll out some colored fondant, cut the letters out and stick them onto your cake.

If you have time, allow the letters to harden for a couple of hours before transferring them to your cake. They are then less likely to bend out of shape.

152
Initial impact

You can use an ornate typeface to select your cake recipient's initials. Try looking in books or magazines for a font you'd like to use.

TRY IT

153 USE CUTTERS DIRECTLY ON THE CAKE

As an alternative to cutting out separate letters, you could simply press the cutters into your cake to leave a written impression in the fondant.

Making fondant figures

Fondant is an ideal medium for making figures, because it is a bit like using edible modeling clay. Children can have fun creating colorful characters—the main problem is usually restricting the amount of fondant they sneakily eat! Guidance on achieving your desired skin tone is given on page 45.

Rolling fondant

When rolling fondant for models, it's best to use a small silicone rolling pin. It is a useful tool for rolling out small sections of fondant for hair and clothing.

 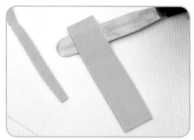 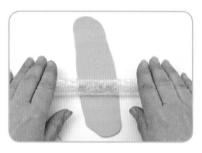

1 Dust your work surface, rolling pin, and fingers with a little confectioners' sugar and roll the fondant out as you would pastry. Use a sharp nonserrated knife or a cutter to cut out the required shapes.

2 To lessen the chances of the fondant stretching when you lift it, slide a palette knife under it to make sure it is not stuck to the board anywhere.

3 If you want to add a pattern to your model's clothes you could consider using a textured rolling pin.

Use a paintbrush for a rolling pin

If you need to roll out a tiny bit of fondant for something like a baby's blanket, but you don't have a small enough rolling pin you can use your paintbrush on its side instead.

Joining fondant

Usually a light dab of water is all that is needed to stick your models together. The water will start to dissolve the sugar in the fondant and form a bond once dried.

 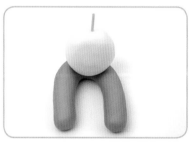

1 Dip a soft paintbrush in water and press it against the side of the dish to remove the excess water so it doesn't drip and leave watermarks in the fondant.

2 To make delicate sections a little more secure, insert a piece of dry spaghetti and reinforce with a dab of water. Don't use toothpicks since this could be dangerous if someone bites into the model.

3 Use other models and even the cake itself to add extra support to your figures. Two characters leaning against each other looks cute, but also means they are less likely to fall over.

Making basic shapes

Many fondant models start out as basic shapes that simply need a little tweaking to add the necessary details to transform them into unique decorations. Don't worry about fingermarks; once you have the shape the fingermarks can be lightly polished out. Always dust your work surface and knead the fondant until smooth before you begin modeling.

◀ Shaping fondant
Knead the fondant lightly to make the surface smooth before shaping.

Ball
The ball is ideal for heads, snowballs, eyes and pumpkins.
1 Dust one of your palms with confectioners' sugar, especially if your hands are warm, then roll the fondant carefully between both palms.
2 Continue to roll the fondant until you have a smooth, round shape.

Egg
An egg shape is useful for heads and animal bodies.
1 Dust one palm with confectioners' sugar and roll the fondant in the palm of your hands to form a ball.
2 Hold your fingers flat and gently press and roll the ball at the same time.
3 The fondant should resemble an egg shape.

Cube
A cube can be used for building blocks or books.
1 Flatten the fondant on four sides to create a rough cube shape.
2 Pinch each corner into a sharp point, but don't indent the flat surface of the cube.
3 You could also use two cake smoothers to flatten two surfaces at a time, moving the cube over and flattening the next two sides until finished.

Sausage
You will use a tapering sausage shape to create legs and arms for your characters.
1 Roll a little fondant into a ball.
2 With your fingers flat, press and roll the ball backward and forward on your work surface.
3 The fondant should spread and become a long sausage shape.

Cone
A cone shape is used for various human and animal body sections.
1 Dust your fingers with a little confectioners' sugar and roll a little fondant into a ball.
2 Gently press and roll on one edge of the ball using one or two fingers. The ball should now resemble a carrot shape.
3 Flatten the base and stand the cone upright.

Heart
A heart shape is great for decorating Valentine's day cupcakes.
1 Dust one palm with confectioners' sugar and roll the fondant to form a ball.
2 Roll the fondant on the edge of your palm to shape into a rough teardrop.
3 Flatten the rough shape between your palms slightly.
4 Use a toothpick to indent the fondant at the top of the heart. Flatten a little further to accentuate the shape.

158

Adding details

It's the little details, such as a link to a recipient's hobby or a favorite item of clothing, that will make your cakes a delight to receive. Adding small details doesn't have to be difficult.

1 Reference a passion or hobby by making a book! Wrap a strip of fondant around three sides of a thick fondant rectangle and write the recipient's interest on the front with food color.

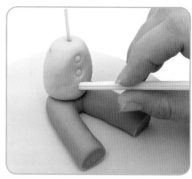

2 Use the tip of a drinking straw to make buttons on your character's clothes, or the tip of a sharp knife to make a line of stitching.

159

Order of work

Make up the different sections of a figure as you go along. For instance, make the legs, then make a ball of fondant for the body and stick that on top of the legs. Next, make the head, and so on. That way the different body parts will be soft enough to gently press and stick together. If you make all the different parts and then try to stick them together at the end, the body bits you made first will have started to dry out and crack when you try to press them into place.

160

Supporting your figures

It may not be the case that you have to rig up complicated internal supports for your figure. Try using the side of the cake for propping your standing figure against. Or you can create a seated figure and sit it on top of the cake or on the edges with its feet dangling over the edge.

Making a basic male figure

The instructions given here are for a very simple model of a man. Feel free to customize him in any way you like. You could do this by adding different hairstyles or expressions. You could even decorate his clothing.

You will need
1¹⁄₂ oz (45 g) blue fondant
1 oz (30 g) white fondant
⁵⁄₈ oz (18 g) flesh-colored fondant
¹⁄₂ oz (15 g) brown fondant
1 strand dry spaghetti
Black food coloring paste
Small nonserrated knife
Paintbrush
Piping nozzle
Toothpick

Start where you see this symbol and work round the steps in numbered order.

4 Roll about ¹⁄₂ oz (15 g) of flesh-colored fondant into a ball for the head and stick it onto the body. Using the edge of a piping nozzle, press a smile into the lower part of the face.

5 Roll ¹⁄₃ oz (10 g) of white fondant into a sausage about 4 in (10 cm) long for the figure's arms. Cut the sausage in half and, with the rounded ends forming the shoulders, lay and stick onto the body.

3 Poke a broken strand of dry spaghetti into the body for extra support. Leave about ¹⁄₂ in (1.5 cm) protruding on which you can slot the head.

6 From a ¹⁄₈ oz (5 g) lump of flesh-colored fondant pull off enough to make three tiny ball shapes. Divide the rest in half and make two ball shapes for hands. Flatten them slightly and stick one on the end of each arm.

2 Roll about 1 oz (30 g) white fondant into an oval shape and stick on top of the body with a light dab of water.

7 Take a small lump of brown fondant for the hair and dip it into a little water. Mush it around in your fingers then spread and stick it onto the head.

1 Begin with the legs and roll about 1¹⁄₂ oz (45 g) of blue fondant into a sausage about 5 in (15 cm) long. Slice off the two rounded ends and bend the sausage into a "U" shape.

8 Stick the three tiny flesh balls in position: One in the middle of the face for the nose and the other two on either side of the head for the ears. Poke the end of a paintbrush into each ear to leave a little hollow.

10 Make two ¹⁄₈ oz (5 g) brown oval shapes for the shoes and stick one onto the end of each leg. Press a line into the sole of each shoe with the back of your knife.

9 Dip the tip of a toothpick into some black food color paste and make two dots for eyes.

162

Making a basic female figure

Customize the hair color and any other characteristics to make the figure resemble the recipient. The lady shown has an open mouth as though she's singing, but you could use the man's smiling mouth if you prefer.

5 Make two small flesh-colored ball shapes for the hands. Flatten them slightly and stick them onto the arms on her lap. One hand should slightly overlap the other.

6 Roll ⅓ oz (10 g) of flesh-colored fondant into a ball for the head and stick it onto the body. Poke the end of a paintbrush into the lower part of the face to make a mouth. Dip the tip of a toothpick into some black food coloring and make two dots for the eyes. Using the tip of a scalpel or craft knife, press three tiny lines either side of the eyes for the eyelashes. Make a tiny flesh-colored ball for the nose and stick it onto the face.

4 Roll about ⅛ oz (5 g) of white fondant into a sausage about 4 in (10 cm) long for the arms. Cut in half and stick onto the body.

3 Thinly roll out about ½ oz (15 g) of pink fondant and cut out a rectangle about 4 in x 1 in (10 in x 3 cm). Dab a little water over the top of the legs and lay the skirt around the waist (it will not meet at the back.)

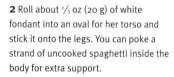

7 For the hair, thinly roll out about ⅓ oz (10 g) of black fondant and cut out a circle shape with a 1½ in (3.5 cm) diameter. Press lines into the disk with the back of your knife and cut it in half. With the rounded sides of the semicircles facing forward, stick the hair onto the head and tweak into position using your paintbrush.

2 Roll about ⅔ oz (20 g) of white fondant into an oval for her torso and stick it onto the legs. You can poke a strand of uncooked spaghetti inside the body for extra support.

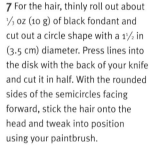

1 Begin with the legs and roll ⅔ oz (20 g) of flesh-colored fondant into a sausage about 7 in (18 cm) long. Bend it into a "U" shape and either place it flat on top of the cake or on the edge with the legs dangling over the side.

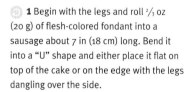

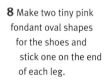

8 Make two tiny pink fondant oval shapes for the shoes and stick one on the end of each leg.

Making a basic baby

Fondant babies are simple to make, especially because you don't need to make any clothing.

2 Press a piping nozzle into the face for the mouth and pull downward. Make two cheeks by pressing the edge of a drinking straw into the fondant on either side of the mouth. Make a tiny white fondant square shape for a single tooth and stick it just inside the mouth. Add a tiny string of black fondant to the top of the head for hair.

3 Add a tiny fondant ball for the nose and two for the ears. Press the end of a paintbrush into each ear to make hollows and, using a toothpick and some black food coloring, make two dots for eyes.

 1 Roll ½ oz (15 g) of flesh-colored fondant into an oval. Make a ⅛ oz (5 g) flesh-colored ball shape for the head and stick it on top.

4 Roll ⅛ oz (5 g) of flesh-colored fondant into a sausage for the legs. Cut it in half and bend the end of each half into an "L" shape to form a foot. Stick one on either side of the body.

5 Make two tiny flesh-colored sausage shapes for arms and stick onto the sides of the torso.

Use a paintbrush for delicate work

Lifting and positioning tiny details like the tooth can be difficult, so try using the tip of your paintbrush to put it in position.

▶ **Making models**
You can either make your models off the cake then carefully lift and stick them in place, or make them in situ on top of the cake.

Grumpy

Eyes: Press the tip of a scalpel or craft knife into the soft fondant three times on either side of the nose.

Mouth: Press the edge of a piping nozzle into the fondant in order to create a turned-down mouth.

Hair: Dip a little fondant in water, roll it around your fingers and press onto the head. Alternatively, color a little buttercream or royal icing and use a dab of that instead.

 165

Getting proportions right

As a general rule any adult figures should be taller than those of children. The heads on children should be bigger in proportion to their bodies than those on adults. Ears and noses should be level and placed approximately halfway down the head.

▼ Hidden expressions

A hand stuck over a smiling mouth makes a character look as though they're really laughing!

 166

Use writing icing

Writing icing is a good choice for adding facial hair to your characters.

 167

Hairstyles and expressions

These head models demonstrate a number of different ways to make hair, eyes, and mouths. The techniques are interchangeable, so you could use a mouth from one model and team it with hair from another. Experiment and find out what suits you, your style and, of course, the cake's recipient.

Smiling

Eyes: Dip the tip of a toothpick into black food coloring and make two dots. Alternatively, paint dots with the tip of a fine paintbrush.

Mouth: Press the edge of a piping nozzle into the fondant and pull downward to produce an open-mouthed smile.

Hair: Cut out a small fondant rectangle. Cut a fringe into one long side and stick around the head.

Sultry

Eyes: Using a fine paintbrush and black food coloring, paint two curved lines onto the face. Paint a "U" shape directly below.

Mouth: Paint an "M" shape below the nose and a short line below that. Paint a shallow "U" shape below the line.

Hair: Make a small fondant rectangle and press lines into it with the back of your knife. Cut the rectangle in half and stick onto the head.

Whistling

Eyes: Make two white fondant balls and flatten them. Stick them in position and make two dots for the pupils using a toothpick and black food coloring.

Mouth: Make a flesh-colored ball shape and slightly squash it into an oval. Press the end of a toothpick into the top of the oval and stick onto the face.

Hair: Make a small fondant rectangle and press lines into it with the back of a knife. Stick it onto the head. Press the back of the knife onto the middle of the head to make a center parting.

Cheeky

Eyes: Make two white fondant balls and flatten them. Stick them onto the head and paint a black food coloring "U" shape onto each eye.

Mouth: Press the edge of a piping nozzle into the fondant. Press the edge of a drinking straw either side of the mouth.

Hair: Place a little black buttercream or royal icing into a piping bag fitted with a number 1 piping nozzle and pipe squiggles all over the head. Alternatively, use a tube of black writing icing.

Yawning

Eyes: Holding a drinking straw at a slight angle, press the edge into the fondant.

Mouth: Press the end of a wooden spoon into the head to leave a deep hollow.

Hair: For very closely shaven hair, lightly paint a little watered-down food coloring onto the head.

Singing

Eyes: Make two tiny white fondant ball shapes and squash them into ovals. Stick onto the head. Make a third flesh-colored oval and cut it in half, stick one half over each eye and paint a black food coloring "U" shape under each eyelid.

Mouth: Press the end of a paintbrush into the fondant and pull gently downward. This will make the face look as though it is either yawning or singing.

Hair: Dip a little fondant in water. Roll it around your fingers and smear it all over the head. Alternatively, color a little buttercream or royal icing and use that instead.

Confused

Eyes: Paint two black food coloring dots onto the head, then paint a short, sloping line on either side of each eye.

Mouth: Paint a black food coloring dot.

Hair: Cut out a small fondant rectangle and cut a fringe along one side. Stick this onto the front of the head and tweak the strands of hair with the tip of a clean paintbrush.

Making fondant animals

Like figures, fondant animals can be as simple or as complicated as you want to make them, and many will have basic simple shapes in common.

168

Reindeer

Christmas wouldn't be Christmas without Rudolph making an appearance somewhere. You could use him on cakes, cupcakes, or even make an icing herd as a central table decoration!

1 Roll about ⅔ oz (20 g) of brown fondant into a thick sausage shape and slice it into four for the legs. Stand them up and stick them next to each other.

8 Finish with a tiny sausage of fondant for a tail. Tweak the end into a point.

2 Roll 1 oz (30 g) of brown fondant into an oval for the body and stick it on top of the legs.

7 Press the end of your paintbrush onto the middle of the antler. The ends should automatically curl up.

3 Make a ⅔ oz (20 g) brown fondant bowling pin shape for the reindeer's head. Pinch a little fondant in the two top corners of the head to make the ears and stick onto the body.

6 Roll a tiny bit of flesh-colored fondant into a little sausage for the antlers. Place a little dab of water in the center of the sausage and stick it onto the head.

4 Use the back of your knife or a circle cutter to press a mouth into the lower part of the body.

5 Add two white oval shapes for eyes and a red one for the nose. Use a toothpick to add two black food coloring dots to the eyes.

169

Work ahead

You can make models well in advance. Keep them in a cardboard cake box away from dust and light until needed.

If you can make this
bowling pin shape ...

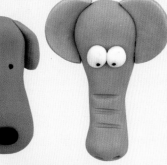

You can make all of these animal heads...

170

Animal head shapes

All these animal head shapes start life as a bowling pin shape, so master
that and away you go. The cat has two ears pinched into one end and is
then bent into a "U" shape. Make two eyes with the end of a drinking
straw, a dot for a nose, and a little tail. Meow!

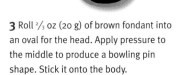

...Plus a cat !

171

Dog

You can alter the fondant colors to
change the dog's appearance, or
add black food color patches.

5 Press a mouth into the lower
part of the head using a circle
cutter or the back of your knife.
Using a toothpick, add two dots of
black food coloring for eyes and a
small black fondant oval for a nose.

4 Divide ⅛ oz (5 g) of brown fondant
into three. Roll one-third into a little
string for the tail and stick it onto the
rear of the dog. Roll the other two pieces
into small sausage shapes and stick them
onto the sides of the head for the ears.

1 Divide 1 oz (30 g) of brown
fondant into four and roll each
quarter into an oval. Stick them
together and press three lines
into the front of each paw with
the back of your knife.

2 Roll 1 oz (30 g) of brown
fondant into an oval for the
body and stick it on the top
of the legs.

You will need
3 oz (90 g) brown fondant
Tiny piece of black fondant
Black food coloring
Sharp nonserrated knife
Paintbrush
Circle cutter (optional)
Toothpick

3 Roll ⅔ oz (20 g) of brown fondant into
an oval for the head. Apply pressure to
the middle to produce a bowling pin
shape. Stick it onto the body.

You will need
2 oz (60 g) green fondant
Tiny piece of white fondant
Black food coloring
Sharp nonserrated knife
Paintbrush
Drinking straw
Circle cutter (optional)
Toothpick

172

Crocodile

Although he won't scare anyone at the party, this easy-to-make crocodile will definitely be a star attraction.

1 Roll 1 oz (30 g) of green fondant into a long tapering sausage shape, about 6 in (15 cm), for the body.

2 Divide about ⅓ oz (10 g) of green fondant into four and make four little sausage shapes for the legs. Stick them into position against the body.

3 Press a couple of lines into each foot with the back of a knife and press scales down the length of the body using the edge of a drinking straw.

7 Add two black dots using food coloring and a toothpick for the eyes and press a few scales into the head with the drinking straw.

4 Roll ⅔ oz (20 g) of green fondant into a bowling pin shape for the head. Use a circle cutter or the back of a knife to press a mouth into the end of the head and add two nostrils using the end of a paintbrush.

5 Make two tiny white fondant oval shapes for the eyes and stick them onto the head.

6 Make two tiny green strings for the eyelids. Bend them into slight "S" shapes and stick one over each eye.

173

Animal textures

There are various ways you can create animal textures and skins. Here are just a few of the most common:

1 Scales
Holding a piping nozzle or a drinking straw at a slight angle, press "U" shapes into the fondant while it's still soft.

2 Fur
Using the back of a knife or the tip of a toothpick, press or drag lines into the fondant while it's still soft and pliable.

3 Feathers
While the fondant is still soft, gently press the tip of a knife into the icing to leave "V"-shaped marks. Alternatively, make little "V"-shaped snips with a small pair of scissors.

4 Animal print
Using a fine paintbrush and some black food color, paint a few oblongs onto the fondant, then paint curved lines on either side of each oblong. You can use this painting method to imitate a whole host of animal prints, not just the leopard print shown here.

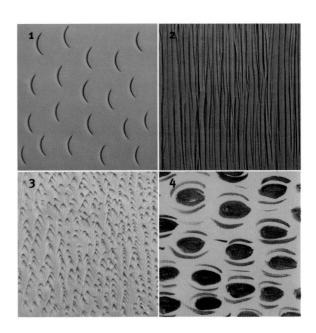

174

Keep an eye on proportions

You can create a whole menagerie of animals to decorate your cake, but keep in mind how they will look together if you want to feature them on the same cake. Carefully plan out the proportions of your animals to ensure you don't have an enormous dog dwarfing a tiny hippo!

175

Animal cake pops

You can use fondant to decorate a chocolate cake pop. Make up the pops and allow to set. Make a small fondant animal head and attach it to the pop with a little melted chocolate or royal icing.

Making simple fondant roses

Roses make great decorations for a cake. It is well worth mastering a few simple ones, even if you are a beginner, because they are so versatile and can be used to celebrate so many occasions. Although it cannot be rolled as thinly as other types of modeling paste, fondant can still be used to make many elegant roses.

▲ A fondant rose is a simple yet elegant way to decorate a cupcake and turn it into something special.

TRY IT

176 SIMPLE RIBBON ROSE CUPCAKES: THREE VARIATIONS
- Pipe a swirl of buttercream onto the top of a cupcake and place the rose on top (see below).
- Cut out a fondant disk and, using a little water or apricot jam, stick it to the top of the cupcake and stick the rose on top.
- Make a cluster of tiny roses. Spread a little royal icing over the cupcake and place the roses on top.

177

Making a ribbon rose

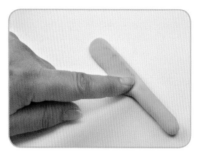

1 Knead about 1 oz (30 g) of fondant until pliable, then roll it out into a long sausage. Press along one long edge of the sausage to flatten. Slide a palette knife under the fondant to make sure it's not sticking to your work surface.

2 Paint a light line of water along the thick edge of the strip then carefully wind the fondant up like a loose bandage. The thick end should form the base. Tweak the petals into position and stand it upright.

3 Thinly roll out a little green fondant. Cut out a simple leaf shape. Press a few veins into it using the back of your knife and stick around the base of the rose.

178

Petalled rose

This is another method for making a slightly more realistic rose. With a little practice you will find that it is still fairly simple to do.

1 Take about 1/3 oz (10 g) of fondant and roll it into a ball. Pinch one side, pull it gently, and flatten it. You will end up with a shape that looks like a tadpole when viewed from above.

2 Wrap the thin flappy bit around the thick portion. You should find a point forming at the top. This will be the center of the rose.

3 Use about 1/8 oz (5 g) of fondant for a petal. Roll it into a ball and pinch it between your fingers to flatten and thin one edge. Dab a little water on the thick base of the petal and wrap the base around the center.

4 Repeat with another petal but allow the edges of the second petal to overlap the first.

5 Make another three petals and place them so that they all overlap each other.

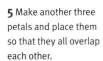

6 Slice off the excess fondant from the base of the rose and gently tweak and position the tips of the petals.

TRY IT

179 **MAKE A CLUSTER**
A cluster of roses around the base and edge of a white fondant-covered cake makes a beautiful centerpiece for any celebratory occasion. Stick the roses into position as you make them so that they mold and fit together neatly. You should only need light dabs of water to secure them in place. Add the leaves afterward and use them to hide any mistakes or unsightly areas of visible rose base.

180

Rose cake pop

Roses are not just for cakes; they work well on cake pops too. Stir a little pink food color paste into some melted white chocolate, dip the pop into the mixture, and decorate with a tiny rose.

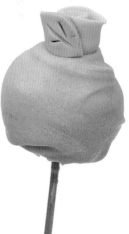

Making flowers with cutters

Nowadays there are hundreds of cutters available to help make creating exotic flowers easy. The majority are either plastic or metal. Although metal will give a slightly cleaner cut, metal cutters can be more expensive and can bend out of shape if not stored carefully.

Five-petal flowers

The five-petal flower cutter is one of the most useful you can buy. Available in various sizes, its simple shape can be used to create three-dimensional flowers as well as bold, flat, cartoon-style blooms that are great for decorating novelty cakes.

Shaped five-petal flower

1 Make little bowls out of aluminum foil for the flowers to sit in while they harden into shape—you'll need enough for the number of flowers you intend to make.

2 Thinly roll out 1 oz (30 g) of colored fondant and cut out the flower shapes. Place a flower into each foil mold and leave them somewhere warm to dry out, preferably overnight.

3 When set, gently dust the center of the flower with a small amount of green edible dusting powder if you wish.

4 Carefully place the flower into position on the cake and pipe a dot of royal icing in the center.

Flat five-petal flowers

You can make a flat version of the five-petal flower. Follow the steps (left), but allow the flowers to harden while flat. You can finish them by either cutting out a small disk for the center using a piping nozzle or pipe a few royal icing dots in the middle.

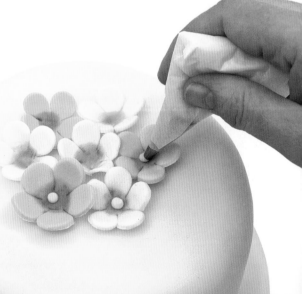

Blossom plunge cutter flowers

These cutters are extremely useful. They create tiny flowers that you can use in many ways. Roll out your fondant and cut out a flower. Press the plunger down to ease the flower out of the cutter and place it into position. As it depresses, the flower will assume a curved shape. Pipe a dot of royal icing or place a tiny fondant ball in the center of the flower to finish.

▲ **Cutter collections**

Cutters can be expensive, so buy them as you need them. A five-petal cutter and a blossom plunge cutter will get you a long way.

TRY IT

184 USING BLOSSOM PLUNGE CUTTER FLOWERS
Here are a number of ways for you to use the flowers created by a blossom plunge cutter.
• Use the flower to hide the seams on piped loops on the side of a cake (see below).
• Make a pretty floral ring around the edges of your cakes and plaques.
• Use a blossom plunge cutter to make a cute hair decoration or miniature bunch of flowers on an icing character.
• Adorn your cupcakes with a tiny bouquet. Pipe a few lines and stick the blossoms on top.
• Decorate your cake pops with them.

▲ **Single blooms**

You don't need a whole bouquet of flowers to turn a simple cake into something special. Often a single flower is enough.

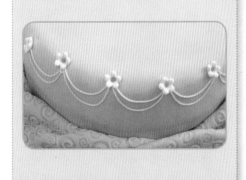

▲ Flaunting foliage

Often overlooked, the humble leaf can be a thing of beauty. A leaf design like this would also look stunning created in autumnal hues.

185

Freehand leaves

The simplest way to make a leaf is to thinly roll out some green fondant and cut out a simple leaf shape using a small, sharp knife. Press a few veins into it using the back of your knife.

If you want the leaf to dry in an irregular position, scrunch up a little aluminum foil and let the leaf dry on that.

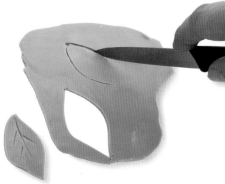

186

Leaf cutters

Cutting out individual leaves by hand can be fiddly and time-consuming, so a couple of different-sized leaf cutters may come in handy. There are many different leaf cutters available. If you are just starting out, rose and ivy cutters are probably the most useful to begin with.

▼ Rose leaf cutter

Thinly roll out a piece of fondant and press the cutter into it to give you your leaf. You can then press it onto a veiner and place it on a former or crumpled aluminum foil to dry in the position you desire.

187 FONDANT IVY

Ivy fronds are an effective way to add elegance to a cake. Paint a wavy line using green food coloring and a fine brush. Add a few curls and stick a few ivy leaves onto the cake using dots of royal icing. You can also dab a little food color in the middle of each leaf. The shade of green used here is called gooseberry.

▶ Veiners

Once you've used your simple open cutter then press your fondant leaf onto a veiner before drying so that it leaves a veined impression.

◀ Ivy leaf cutter

Some plunge cutters have veiners incorporated into the cutter so that veins are superimposed onto the leaf or flower as you cut it out.

188

Coordinating your table

If you are making cakes for a special event it can be a nice touch to coordinate the cakes with the table décor. This can be done easily by placing a simple fondant flower that matches the napkins, plates, or flowers on top of your cake. Another method is to take a look at the plethora of colored cake liners and delicate cake wrappers that are now available to stand your cupcakes in. They can immediately transform a humble tea table into an elegant work of art.

Applying fresh flowers

Fresh flowers can be used on cakes, but should be used with caution since some flowers are poisonous and therefore unsuitable. The flowers should be pesticide-free and, to avoid any sort of contamination, they should never come into contact with the surface of the cake.

▶ Food-safe lavender is available to buy and can actually be used for flavoring your cakes as well as for a simple decoration.

189

Flowers to use and avoid

Here is a list of some of the more common flowers presently considered safe and unsafe for use on cakes. You should always do your research thoroughly and check with your florist first before incorporating flowers into your design.

SAFE FLOWERS	POISONOUS FLOWERS
Apple blossom	Anemone
Begonia	Calla lily
Cornflower	Clematis
Daisy (English)	Daffodil
Freesia	Delphinium
Geranium	Frangipani
Hibiscus	Gloriosa lily
Honeysuckle	Hydrangea
Impatiens	Iris
Lavender	Ivy
Pansy	Ranunculus
Rose	Poppy
Tulip	Sweet pea
Violet	Wisteria

190

Making crystallized flowers

Crystallized flowers make spectacular decorations for celebration cakes.

Paint the petals, leaves, or whole flower with gum Arabic, egg white or stock syrup then dip in superfine sugar. Allow the flowers to dry overnight on a wire rack. Crystallized flowers are not edible and unless you're using food-safe flowers they should not be placed directly on the cake.

191

Wiring flowers

Push a 22-gauge or stub wire into the stem of the flower, making sure that it is pushed in sufficiently to hold the flower. Tape over with half-width florist tape. Once wired, the flower stalks are pushed into a flower pick (see opposite) and inserted into the cake.

192

Wiring a spray

By wiring the stalks of flowers and foliage in a bouquet you can create an attractive arrangement that you know will stay securely in its place.

1 Tape together three flowers using half-width florist tape. Start with the smallest flower and gradually add a little height to each of the other two. The largest flower will form the focal point of the spray so it needs to be higher than any of the other flowers in the spray. The three stems are joined together to form a handle to the spray. The focal flower should be positioned approximately two-thirds in length from the flowers or foliage at the tip of the spray, with the remaining third of plant materials wired in behind the focal flower.

2 Now add your next flowers, again starting with the smallest flower toward the tip of the spray. Bend and tape each wired stem as you add them to the spray. Cut off any excess wire as you work to reduce the bulk of the handle. Add wired leaves to fill in the large spaces between the flowers. Soften the edges and add length to the spray using wired stems.

3 Add loops and trails of decorative paper-covered wire. Stand back from the spray and take another look at the whole display to check if anything needs repositioning. Keep the spray of flowers in a cool place until it is needed—it is usually best to assemble the flowers the day before or preferably on the morning of the day they are needed to ensure that they are fresh.

193

Picking your flowers

Flowers should never be poked into the cake itself. A flower pick is a food-safe plastic tube that is pushed into the cake. They can be bought from cake decorating stores. Your posy of flowers stands within the pick and doesn't touch the cake.

1 Sterilize the pick by wiping it with clear alcohol. Decide where the spray of flowers is to be positioned and carefully insert the pick into the cake. It is best to have the top section of the pick showing so that it can be retrieved easily prior to the cake being cut.

2 Insert the handle of a wired spray of fresh flowers into the pick.

Marzipan

Marzipan, or almond paste as it is sometimes called, is a thick, slightly grainy sweet dough made from almonds. It is surprisingly versatile and in many cases can be used as a substitute for fondant if you prefer the taste. It can be used both to cover cakes and make detailed models.

Marzipan recipe

Marzipan is easily obtainable from cake-decorating stores, supermarkets, and online, or you can make your own. Unlike most other marzipan recipes, the eggs are cooked in this one. This reduces the possibility of food poisoning due to salmonella. The marzipan should be used as soon as possible, but it can be stored for a couple of days in the fridge double wrapped in small plastic food bags or plastic wrap.

Ingredients
1 egg plus an extra yolk
4 oz (110 g) superfine sugar
4 oz (110 g) confectioners' sugar
8 oz (225 g) ground almonds
A few drops of almond essence

FIX IT

195 KEEP MARZIPAN FIRM
The marzipan will firm up as it cools but if it still feels too soft, knead in a little more confectioners' sugar.

1 Put the eggs and both types of sugar into a heatproof bowl. Stand the bowl over a pan of hot water and whisk until the mixture becomes thick and creamy.

2 Remove the bowl from the heat and add a few drops of almond essence. Stir in the almonds and knead into a ball.

Working with marzipan: Basic rules

Marzipan is easy to work with, but there are some simple rules to remember:

- Once it is out of its package marzipan will begin to dry out and harden, so keep any unused marzipan double wrapped in small resealable food bags. Store-bought marzipan does not need to be kept in the fridge.
- Knead and roll the marzipan out on confectioners' sugar, not cornflour, because this can react unfavorably with the marzipan.
- If your marzipan is quite hard, you can soften it in the microwave for a few seconds. Repeat if necessary. You must be careful, because marzipan contains oils that can get very hot and burn. Heat in short increment bursts rather than one long blast.
- You will only need water to stick marzipan models together. Use a little cooled boiled water if possible.
- You always need to cover a fruitcake with marzipan before covering it with fondant or royal icing to keep the moisture in the cake.
- When covering a cake with marzipan use jam to stick it to the cake and not buttercream since the marzipan can react to buttercream. Apricot jam is a good choice because it has a mild taste.

- Although not necessary, you can put a layer of marzipan over a pound cake before covering it with fondant. Double covering like this makes achieving a smooth finish much easier.
- If, after covering with marzipan, you plan to cover the cake with fondant, "paint" the marzipanned cake with cooled boiled water to make a sticky surface to hold the fondant in place. You will not have to do this if covering the marzipan with royal icing.

Preparing for marzipan

Apricot jam should be heated in the microwave or in a heatproof bowl over simmering water to boiling point, then put through a strainer before spreading to remove any apricot skin. This is because occasionally chemicals in the apricot skin can cause the marzipan to "blow" (pull away slightly from the sides.)

Coloring marzipan

Marzipan can easily be colored using food pastes in the same way as fondant. However, even "natural" marzipan is not pure white, so you will need more color than you would with fondant to get the shade that you want.

◀ **Presenting marzipan models**
If you want to gift your marzipan models you can place them in their own petit-four liners.

199

Covering a fruitcake with marzipan

Traditionally fruitcakes are covered with a layer of marzipan before being covered with a layer of fondant or royal icing.

Quantity guide

As with fondant, the amount of marzipan you require to cover your cake will vary slightly, depending on how thick you like your marzipan. Here is a rough guide for different-sized cakes.

MARZIPAN QUANTITY GUIDE

		6 in (15 cm)	7 in (18 cm)	8 in (20 cm)	9 in (23 cm)	10 in (25 cm)	11 in (28 cm)	12 in (30 cm)
SQUARE PAN		6 in (15 cm)	7 in (18 cm)	8 in (20 cm)	9 in (23 cm)	10 in (25 cm)	11 in (28 cm)	12 in (30 cm)
ROUND PAN	6 in (15 cm)	7 in (18 cm)	8 in (20 cm)	9 in (23 cm)	10 in (25 cm)	11 in (28 cm)	12 in (30 cm)	
MARZIPAN	1 lb 2 oz (500 g)	1 lb 6 oz (650 g)	1 lb 12 oz (800 g)	2 lb (900 g)	2 lb 8 oz (1.1 kg)	3 lb (1.4 kg)	3 lb 8 oz (1.6 kg)	4 lb (1.8 kg)

200

Marzipanning a fruitcake for fondant

Since a fondant-covered cake has gently rounded edges and corners, both square and round cakes are covered in the same way—all at one time.

1 Slice the top off the cake to level it if necessary, turn it upside down and place it on the cake board.

2 Fill any holes on what is now the top of the cake with little balls of marzipan. If there is a gap between the base of the cake and the board, press a sausage of marzipan into it.

3 If you wish to add a little alcohol to the cake, pierce the top a few times with a toothpick and drizzle 1 tbsp (15 ml) of brandy over the top of the cake.

6 Lift and place the marzipan over the cake. Smooth the top and sides and trim away any excess from around the base. Ideally, you should run a cake smoother over the cake to finish.

4 Place 2 tbsp (30 ml) of apricot jam into a heatproof bowl and either place over a pan of simmering water to heat it to boiling point or place it in the microwave for a few seconds. "Paint" the jam over the outside of the cake with a pastry brush.

5 Dust your work surface with confectioners' sugar and knead and roll out the marzipan.

201

Marzipanning a fruitcake for royal icing

If you want to achieve crisp edges and corners with your royal icing you will need to cover your fruitcake in sections. If, however, you plan on a swirly snow scene, then cover it using the simpler method shown opposite.

Round cake

Before you put jam on the cake, measure its height and circumference and make a note of the measurements.

1 If necessary, level the cake and paint boiled apricot jam onto the top of it. Knead and roll out about a third of the marzipan. It should not be any thinner than ¼ in (5 mm). Place the cake upside down onto the marzipan. Cut away the excess with a sharp knife and reuse it for the sides.

2 Turn the cake the right way up and stand it on the board. Paint jam around the sides and knead and roll out the remaining marzipan. Cut out a long strip as wide as the height of the cake and as long as the circumference.

4 The cake must be as smooth as possible because any bumps will show through the royal icing. Leave to dry for a minimum of 48 hours before adding the royal icing.

3 Roll the strip up a bit like a bandage and unwind it around the cake. Carefully run over the cake with a cake smoother.

Square cake

1 If necessary, level the cake and paint boiled apricot jam onto the top of it. Roll out about a third of the marzipan and place the cake upside down on top. Cut around the edges and place the cake the right way up on the cake board.

2 Measure the length and width of the cake and paint jam around the sides. Cut out four marzipan strips using the measurements and stick them around the sides.

3 Smooth the sides and top of the cake. It must be as neat and crisp as possible. Leave the cake for at least 48 hours before adding the royal icing.

202

Let the cake dry out before icing

If you have time, let your covered fruitcake stand for a day or so before covering it with fondant or royal icing. This is to allow it to dry out and reduce the chances of oils from the marzipan seeping into the outside covering.

203

Covering a pound cake

You can cover a pound cake in the same way that you would a fruitcake, but make sure that you level the cake before beginning so that you end up with an even surface to decorate.

204

Marzipan models

As well as covering cakes, marzipan can be used for creating models, cake toppers, and even decorations for cake pops. If it can be made in fondant, it can be made in marzipan. The only thing you will not be able to do is to achieve a bright white finish. Stick the components together with light dabs of water.

Marzipan Teddy

A teddy is simple to make. If you don't like the taste of marzipan you can use the same instructions to make a teddy out of fondant.

6 To finish use a toothpick and black food coloring to make dots for his eyes, nose and mouth and poke a hollow into each ear using the end of your paintbrush.

5 Make two tiny ball shapes for his ears and an oval for his muzzle. Stick all three components in place.

4 Make a ¹/₃ oz (10 g) sausage shape for his arms. Cut it in half and stick one arm on either side of his body.

▼ **Teddy toys**
If you're making a fondant child, you could make a miniature version of this teddy to go with it.

You will need
2 ¹/₂ oz (70 g) marzipan
Small nonserrated knife
Paintbrush
Black food coloring paste

FIX IT

205 STOP THE MARZIPAN FROM STICKING

When working with marzipan use a little confectioners' sugar to stop your fingers from getting sticky and the marzipan sticking to your work surface. You can use a dusting bag (see below) to dust your work surface. Any dusty sugar marks can be wiped away with a damp paintbrush when your model is finished.

1 Make a 1 oz (30 g) oval for his body and stand upright.

2 Make a ¹/₃ oz (10 g) ball for his head and stick on top.

3 Make a ¹/₂ oz (15 g) sausage shape for his legs. Cut it in half and bend the end of each leg into an "L" shape and stick around the base of his body. Poke the end of your paintbrush into the soles of his feet to add a little detail.

206

Making a dusting bag

A dusting bag allows you to dust your work surface with confectioners' sugar but in a measured and controlled way without filling your kitchen with a sugary cloud. You can make a dusting bag using a little square of muslin. Put a little confectioners' sugar in the center. Gather up the sides and, leaving a little room at the top so the sugar can move about, secure with an elastic band or a little ribbon. To release the sugar, tap the bag on your work surface.

207

Miniature fruit and vegetables

Miniature fruits are easy to model and make great gifts.

Apple
Roll 1 oz (30 g) of green marzipan into a ball shape. Make a tiny brown marzipan sausage shape for the stalk and press it into the top of the apple. Dust a little red edible dusting powder onto one side to finish.

Pear
This is made in the same way as the apple, but instead of a ball shape roll the marzipan into a longer oval shape and squeeze the middle slightly.

Banana
Color 1 oz (45 g) of yellow marzipan and divide it into four. Roll each quarter into a tapering sausage shape. Using black food color, paint a couple of thin lines down the side of each banana and make a black ball for the seam at the top.

Grapes
Make a number of green or purple marzipan oval shapes and pile them together in a triangular formation. Make a thin brown sausage shape for the stalk.

Oranges
Roll 1 oz (30 g) of orange marzipan into a ball. Press a few shallow lines into the top. Press the orange gently against a fine grater to add a bit of texture and insert a dried clove for the detail at the top of the orange.

Carrot
A miniature carrot looks great on a carrot cake! Roll a little orange marzipan into a carrot shape. Press a couple of lines across it with the back of your knife. Make a green marzipan triangle, score some partial cuts into the thick end of the triangle and stick the triangle to the carrot.

▼ **Fruits of the forest**
Marzipan fruit will work really well nestled among fall leaf decorations.

TRY IT

208 CHOCOLATE-DIPPED MARZIPAN POPS
- Make a ball of marzipan. Dip the tip of a lollipop stick into melted chocolate and stick it into the marzipan ball. Allow it to set, then dip the marzipan pop into more melted chocolate. Add some sprinkles or anything else that takes your fancy.
- Alternatively, cut out a marzipan shape and dip that into chocolate. Letters are fun, especially if you are having a party. Everyone can have his or her own initial. Allow the letters to harden on their stick before dipping to lessen the chances of the letters sagging and bending.

3 Buttercream

A simple mixture of butter, confectioners' sugar, and a little water plus a hint of flavoring—if you wish—buttercream is a very simple and quick cake frosting to put together. It is also extremely versatile; not only can you use it for filling and coating your cakes, but you can also use it for piping and to create all sorts of decorations and effects.

Making your own buttercream

Buttercream is a very simple type of cake covering to make at home. To save time you could whip it up while your cake is baking and store it in the fridge until it's needed.

 209

Buttercream recipe

This recipe is quick and easy to put together. The vanilla essence is optional, it is not essential, but it does lift the taste of the buttercream and make it into something a little special.

Ingredients
8 oz (250 g) butter (softened)
1 lb 2 oz (500 g) confectioners' sugar
1 tbsp hot water
1 tsp vanilla essence

1 Beat the butter with a wooden spoon until it is light and fluffy.

2 Stir in the sugar, hot water, and vanilla extract. Beat well until light and smooth. Add a little more liquid or sugar, as needed, to adjust the consistency. If you would prefer to use a mixer, place all the ingredients in the bowl and bind together on a slow speed then increase the speed and mix until light and fluffy.

 210

Christmas fun

Make two simple fondant reindeers (see page 84) and stand them in white icing "snow." The fir trees are green cone-shaped fondant. Pop a green cone on a skewer and make tiny little snips with a pair of scissors to create the branches. Then dust with confectioners' sugar (for snow effect).

Ingredients
2 sachets (4 tsp/20 ml) dried egg white powder
6 fl oz (180 ml) water
8 cups (1 kg) confectioners' sugar
2 tsp (10 ml) glycerine (optional)
2 tsp (10 ml) lemon juice (optional)

1 First ensure the bowl of the food mixer is thoroughly clean and grease-free. Tip the sugar and egg white powder into the bowl and stir together.

2 Add the water and mix into the sugar on a slow speed. It should become a thick paste. If it is thick and crumbly add a few more drops of water.

3 Leave the mixer to beat the icing on a slow speed for 5–10 minutes. When the icing is sleek, glossy, and standing up in peaks it is ready.

4 Add glycerine and lemon if using.

5 Place the royal icing into a plastic container and cover with a sheet of plastic wrap placed directly on top of the icing to stop it crusting over. Put the lid onto the container. Always keep it sealed when not in use.

Royal icing recipe

Royal icing is a hard white icing traditionally used over a covering of marzipan on Christmas fruitcakes and wedding cakes. When modeling, it can be used as an excellent "glue" to help attach large or heavy pieces. It can be textured into peaks, smoothed out to give a perfectly flat surface and piped into amazing shapes, such as coils, lines, shells, and flowers, and is sometimes used for hair on figures.

Royal icing can be bought ready-made, but it is easy to make at home using a food mixer, confectioners' sugar, and egg white or dried egg white powder (meringue powder). Though egg white is the traditional ingredient, royal icing is more commonly made with dried egg white because as it is the safer option. If you are using royal icing to coat the cake, add a little glycerine to stop it turning rock-hard. If the iced fruitcake is to be stored for a long time you can also add a little lemon juice to stop the icing from yellowing.

Royal icing made with fresh egg white should be used within 2 days. If you used dried egg white, it can be stored sealed in a plastic container in the fridge for up to 2 weeks. Stir it thoroughly before use.

Soft white icing

Buttercream is a wonderful frosting, but it is an off-white cream color, which isn't always appropriate. Occasionally you will need to make a design that requires a soft white icing—for a Christmas snow scene for example. In this situation use the buttercream recipe given opposite, but substitute white vegetable shortening for the butter. These are available with no hydrogenated oils, no artificial colorings, and no preservatives. Vegetable shortening will produce a soft white icing that you can use in exactly the same way as buttercream. It produces a very sweet icing. You can add a few drops of vanilla essence if you wish.

Store-bought flavorings

There are many flavorings and essences that you can buy to add a little drama to your buttercream—peppermint, lemon, and almond to name but a few. Usually "essences" are more concentrated and stronger than flavorings, so you would need to add slightly less; however, it is all a question of taste. Add a few drops, stir it in, and taste a little. If it's too weak, add a little more.

214

Getting the right consistency

Depending on what you'll be using your buttercream for, you may want to adjust its stiffness. The recipe given on page 104 will produce a soft, spreadable buttercream, which is ideal for covering a cake. Fresh soft buttercream like this is also ideal for piping flowers or shells around the top edge or the base of a cake. If you want to use buttercream for piping with small writing nozzles you will need to thin the buttercream so that it flows through the nozzle more easily. Stir 1 tsp (5 ml) of hot water into a small bowl of buttercream. Use hot rather than cold water, because cold water will start to set the buttercream and will not mix in as smoothly.

215

Catering for everyone

The buttercream recipe given on page 104 does not contain milk. Since butter is basically the fat from the milk, it only contains traces of lactose. Those who suffer from lactose intolerance can usually cope with buttercream, but please do check and ask the recipient of the cake beforehand because people suffer different levels of sensitivity. As an alternative, you could substitute a vegetable or soya margarine for the butter.

▶ **Chocolate delights**
Chocolate buttercream can be used both to fill and decorate an elegant cake.

TRY IT

 217 COLOR EFFECTS
Fun effects are easy to create with buttercream. You could try placing some contrasting colored dollops of frosting on your cake and swirling them together. Alternatively, place two different colors into a piping bag and create a two-toned effect on your cupcakes.

 218

Coloring buttercream

It is easy to color buttercream so you can coordinate your cakes and decorations. Here are a few hints and tips to help you get good results.

Pastes and gels

Buttercream can be colored using food color pastes or gels. These are more concentrated than liquid colors and won't make the icing runny. Add a few dabs with a toothpick and stir the color in.

Bear in mind that buttercream is a pale, cream color so some colors may become a little distorted—pale blue, for example, may look somewhat greenish. If you want a true pale color, consider using the soft white icing recipe (see page 105) with white vegetable shortening instead.

Natural colors

Some ingredients add both color and taste to your buttercream. Cocoa or coffee will tint the buttercream brown. Jellies too can add color as well as flavor. Stir a spoonful into the buttercream to produce a pinkish hue.

 219

Taste and texture

It's possible to alter the texture of your buttercream as well as the taste. Stir in a handful of dried coconut, crushed mint candies, or chocolate chips. If you just want a bit of crunch in your filling, add some superfine sugar.

 220

Storing and freezing

If you are not going to use your buttercream immediately it can be stored in a plastic food box in the fridge for a week. Alternatively, it can be frozen for a month. Defrost at room temperature for a couple of hours and give it a stir before use. Do not refreeze buttercream that has been defrosted.

 221

Freezing decorations

Because you can freeze buttercream, you can create decorations (see pages 122–125) in advance of when you need them. This is useful if you're decorating on a large scale. Keep them flat in a freezer-safe box until required. When ready, place your frozen decorations straight onto your prepared buttercreamed cake so they don't lose their shape and are easy to handle. As they defrost they will adhere to the cake beneath.

222

Freeze the whole cake

Because you can freeze both cake and buttercream, you can actually freeze a whole buttercream-covered cake. Carefully cover it with plastic wrap and freeze. Allow it to defrost overnight—it will take anywhere from 5 to 12 hours, depending on the room temperature. Condensation may form on the outside of the cake as it defrosts. This is normal and will evaporate as the cake warms up. You cannot freeze a fondant-covered cake.

Frosting a cake with buttercream

Whether you ultimately plan to cover your cake with fondant or a thick layer of buttercream, the first few steps are the same. Tips on leveling your cake and removing the crust are given on pages 26–27.

223

Filling your cake

Before you coat the outside of the cake you need to fill the inside by slicing the cake into layers (see page 27). However, sometimes you may find that the layers don't go back together quite as well as you'd like. Here's a neat trick to ensure the layers are replaced in exactly the same position they were cut.

1 Make a vertical buttercream mark on the side of the cake before you cut it.

2 Slice the cake into layers.

3 Place the bottom layer into position on the board and add stock syrup if you wish (see page 19). Spread buttercream over the base layer.

4 Place the second layer on top, lining up the buttercream marks. Repeat the procedure if your cake has three layers.

▲ **Ready for anything**
Once your cake has been covered with a thick coat of fresh buttercream it is ready for you to decorate in any way you wish.

224

Don't overfill

Don't overfill the layers if you know your cake is to be covered with a heavy layer of fondant. If you do, you may find bulges appearing once the cake is covered and it settles. The ideal amount of buttercream filling is about $\frac{1}{4}$ in (5 mm) thick. A jam filling would be less than this.

225

Not filling with buttercream?

If you want to fill your cake with cream or fruit, you may find it useful to pipe a buttercream dam $\frac{1}{4}$ in (5 mm) from the edge of the cake to contain your filling. This will prevent any oozing.

226

Sides first

After filling the cake, coat the sides of it with buttercream before you do the top. This allows you to hold the top of the cake steady with your other hand and not get too sticky.

Crumb coating

Once the cake is assembled you need to coat the outside. It is easy to dislodge crumbs when coating a pound cake, which, if you're planning on using buttercream can ruin its appearance. To prevent this you need to apply what is called a crumb coat. If you are covering the cake with fondant, you will only need to coat the cake once with buttercream.

- Spread a thin coating of buttercream over the sides and top of the cake.
- Place it into the refrigerator for 15 minutes or so. This is called setting up. This is not necessary if you're covering the cake with fondant because you need the buttercream soft to "glue" the fondant in place.
- Remove the cake. The first thin layer should now have hardened and should stop crumbs escaping when you spread a second, thicker buttercream coating over the cake.

◄ Early stages
The cake beneath the crumb coating is still visible but will be hidden once the second coat is applied.

Second coating

If you want to achieve a smooth buttercream finish, use a turntable, a palette knife and a scraper. These three pieces of equipment will make things easier. However, all is not lost if you don't—there are alternative methods. Make sure that the buttercream you are to work with is soft and creamy, so that it spreads easily over the cake without tearing it. The cake should already have a crumb coating (see above) in place.

1 Place a large spoonful of buttercream on top of the cake and, using the palette knife, carefully spread it over the top of the cake. Your palette knife should be flat, and you will need to spin the turntable as you go.

2 Roughly spread some buttercream around the sides until they are all coated. Hold the cake scraper vertically against the cake and spin the turntable. You should be left with smooth sides around the cake.

3 You will now have some unsightly buttercream pointing skyward at the edges of the cake. Using a clean palette knife and holding it flat, gently coax a small section toward the middle of the cake, slowly spinning the turntable with your other hand. Scrape the buttercream off the palette knife and repeat all the way around the edges of the cake.

FIX IT

229 NO CAKE SCRAPER?
If you don't have a cake scraper hold a clean palette knife vertically against the cake instead. In a real emergency you could use a clean ruler.

TRY IT

230 **ALTERNATIVE WAY TO A SMOOTH FINISH**
Another traditional way to get a smooth finish on buttercream is with a palette knife and a jug of boiling water. The buttercream must be soft so that it won't damage the cake's surface. Crumb coat the cake as shown on page 109, and then spread a thicker, second coating over the cake. Dip the knife into the hot water for a few seconds, then use it to spread the icing over the cake. Repeat, dipping the knife as necessary. The heat will soften the buttercream and the water should stop it from sticking to the knife.

 231

Frosting mini cakes

The principles of coating mini cakes with buttercream are the same as for big cakes. Cover them with a crumb coating first, let them set in the fridge, then spread buttercream over the top and sides.

 232

Cake board turntable

If you don't have a turntable, take a clean cake board that is smaller than the one being used for the cake you are decorating and place it under the stationary cake. You should now be able to turn the larger cake board easily.

FIX IT

233 **NO TURNTABLE?**
If you don't have a turntable, hold the scraper or palette knife vertically and move that around the stationary cake. Be warned, it's a little more difficult to achieve a perfectly smooth surface this way, but unless you are entering a competition the results will still be delicious!

234 **A LESS THAN PERFECT COATING?**
If your perfectly smooth cake looks... well, less than perfectly smooth, don't despair. Run a decorative scraper around the side of the cake to create a pattern or press some small sweets into the frosting instead. You can also hide many a mistake under some piping swirls!

▶ **Vanishing act**
A decorative scraper can transform an imperfectly buttercreamed cake.

235

Best approaches for frosting cupcakes

The big, fat spoonful method
This is the easiest way to decorate a cupcake!

1 Take 1 tsp (15 ml) of buttercream and, using a second teaspoon, scoop it off the first spoon onto the top of the cupcake.

2 Use the back of a clean teaspoon or a palette knife to spread it over the cupcake.

Traditional, swirly piped method
For this you will need a pastry bag or large piping bag fitted with a large star nozzle.

1 Starting from the outside of the cupcake, squeeze the bag and pipe a swirl around the top of the cake. Continue in a circular motion, gradually moving the piping nozzle toward the center of the cupcake.

2 To finish, gently press the piping nozzle into the center of the cake, release pressure on the bag and pull upward. As the buttercream breaks away it should leave a short tail in the icing.

Working out from the center
You can also pipe in reverse, starting from the center of the cupcake.

1 Begin piping your buttercream from the center of your cupcake.

2 Work in a circular motion toward the outside of the cake. This will create an inverted central peak.

▶ **Buttercream bouquet**
Piping outward from the center of the cupcake will create beautiful frosting roses.

Creating different buttercream finishes

There are many different effects you can create with buttercream. Demonstrated here are some of the most popular and versatile.

Stars

Place a star nozzle into your piping bag and half fill the bag with buttercream. Squeeze a little icing through the nozzle onto the cake, then release the pressure. Pull the bag upward and away from the cake. It should leave behind a little star shape on the cake. Continue on the rest of the cake.

Ridges

Cover the cake just as you would if you were giving it a smooth coating. Hold your palette knife almost flat and draw the end of it lightly across the top and sides. This should create a ridged effect. The ridges around the sides of the cake can be vertical or horizontal.

Decorative scraper effects

There are many decorative cake scrapers available, and they can be used to create all sorts of effects on the sides of your cakes. To use a scraper, hold it upright with its base resting on the board and slowly spin the turntable. The scraper should leave an impression behind in the buttercream. If you move the scraper slowly up and down as you revolve the turntable you can create a zigzag pattern.

Quilted icing

To create a quilted effect, first cover the cake with buttercream and get it as smooth as you can. Allow the cake to begin to crust over for a few minutes, and then, using a ruler or straight edge, press diagonal lines into the buttercream.

TRY IT

 STAR BORDER
To pipe a star border, place 2–3 tbsp (30–45 ml) of buttercream into a piping bag fitted with a star nozzle. Holding the bag vertically at the edge of the cake, squeeze a little buttercream out of the nozzle. Release the pressure on the bag and poke the tip gently into the star and pull away. Make another star next to the first one and repeat all the way around the edge of the cake. The larger the star nozzle the fewer stars you will have to pipe. If you are worried about making a mistake you may find it useful to practice piping on a board first.

241

Piped rosettes

This is a quick way to cover either a large cake or a simple cupcake. You will need a large, open star nozzle, such as a 1M—the bigger the nozzle the larger the rosettes. First squeeze out a little buttercream for the center of the rosette, then move the nozzle around in a spiraling motion, allowing the buttercream to fall and build up the rosette. If you are piping onto a large cake, start by piping the rosettes around the base of the cake; then pipe a second layer and continue up the sides and over the top to the center of the cake.

242

Cornelli

Cornelli are piped squiggles. They are fairly easy to create and, like dots, will detract the eye from any imperfections in the cake's surface.

Mix a little water into the buttercream before piping cornelli to make it easier to pipe. This way it will flow through the small piping nozzle more freely.

Cover the cake with buttercream and get it as smooth as you can. Place some buttercream in a bag fitted with a number 2 piping nozzle and pipe squiggles over the cake.

TRY IT

243

DIPPED CAKE EFFECT
Make three or four bowls of colored buttercream in shades of your chosen color. Pipe one or two lines of rosettes around the base of the cake using the darkest shade. Remove the piping nozzle, wash it, and put it into a second piping bag. Pipe another line or two of rosettes above the first ones, using the middle shade of buttercream. Finally, finish covering the cake using the lightest shade. You can fill any holes or seams with piped stars in the relevant shades.

Piping with buttercream

Many of the piped ideas shown in this section can also be produced using royal icing, which, unlike buttercream, dries to a hard, brittle finish. Most decorators would use buttercream when piping onto a cake covered with buttercream and royal icing on a cake covered with fondant. This is to stop the oil from the buttercream bleeding out and staining the fondant, especially if the weather is very warm.

 244

Piping syringes

The buttercream goes into the syringe part and the nozzle screws onto the outside. A plunger is depressed to force the buttercream out through the nozzle.

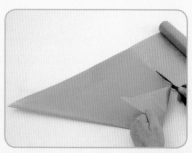

 245

Piping bags

You can buy ready-made piping bags or make your own. There are advantages to both types. It is definitely worth investing in a couple of large, strong piping (pastry) bags that you can use to pipe large quantities of buttercream without fear of the bag splitting along the seams. You can also buy small, disposable piping bags to save on cleaning, or you can make your own. It's all a matter of choice.

1 Take a sheet of parchment paper and fold one corner up to create a triangle shape.

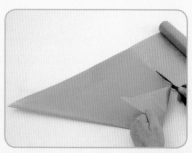

2 Cut the parchment paper to form a square.

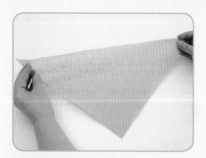

3 Cut along the crease to create two triangles (these will make two piping bags).

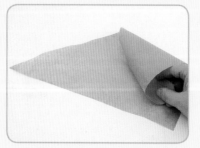

4 Take one of the triangles, pick up one of the corners, and fold it up and around to the apex of the triangle.

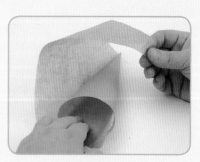

5 Holding this in place, bring the other side around and secure it by folding the parchment paper over the top.

Piped effects without a nozzle

You can use a homemade piping bag to create some simple piped effects without a nozzle by altering the size and shape of the section of paper you snip off the end of the bag. Be sure to squeeze a little icing at a time out of the bag, release the pressure, and pull away.

- Cut a small triangle out of the end of the bag to create a simple petal shape or ridged scroll pattern.
- Cut the tip of the bag into a point and you can create leaf shapes.

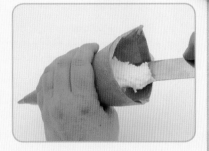

6 Cut the end of the bag off, and drop the decorating tip into the bag. Be careful how much you cut off the end of the bag, otherwise the tip may drop out or be pushed out once you start icing.

7 Fill the piping bag with icing using a palette knife. Do not overfill the bag; keep at least one-third empty.

8 Fold the top of the bag over and push the icing down into the bag, which will keep it from escaping out of the top when you begin to pipe.

FIX IT

248 NO PIPING NOZZLE?
Don't worry, simply make up a piping bag, place the icing inside and close the bag. Snip a tiny triangle off the tip of the bag and pipe through that.

Couplers

Some piping systems come with couplers to make attaching the nozzles easy and secure. The coupler goes inside the piping bag and the nozzle screws on from the outside. The advantage to this system is that you can change the style of piping nozzle without having to delve through a messy piping bag of buttercream to get at it.

Filling your piping bag

Put the buttercream into the bag using a palette knife and clasp it through the bag. As you withdraw the knife, the icing should slide off and stay neatly inside the bag.

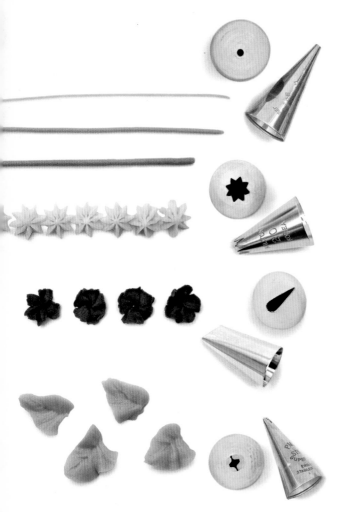

The most useful piping nozzles

There are many different piping nozzles available, and they all have different functions. They are usually numbered.

Numbers 1, 2, and 3

These have plain round holes at their tip and are used for writing and piping fine detail—the smaller the number, the smaller the hole. They can also be used for piping plain shells or scrolls.

Star nozzles

These are available in different sizes and have a zigzag edge, which produces a serrated line of piping. Small star nozzles can be used for piping fine decorative scrolls or edging around cake bases. Larger star nozzles can be used for piping enormous swirls on cupcakes. The star nozzle can also be used for creating simple piped flowers, such as roses.

Flower petal nozzles

A petal nozzle has an elongated, tear-shaped opening. It allows you to create a number of different flowers, including simple blossoms and roses. Petal nozzles are available in various sizes. The larger the petal nozzle, the larger the flower it will create.

Leaf nozzles

It is definitely worth buying a leaf nozzle, as these can be used to create both leaves on piped flowers and to create large leaf shapes on novelty cakes if required.

Alternative uses for piping nozzles

A piping nozzle is not just for piping. Among other things, you can use them to create fondant disks to stand candles in, make smiles and frowns on your fondant models, add scales on fondant animals, and much more.

251

Polka-dot cupcakes

This easy effect is created by piping with colored cake batter.

TRY IT

252   COLORING ALTERNATIVES For an even more dramatic effect, make the cupcake a different color from the dots.

1 Make the cake batter and place a couple of heaping tablespoons into a separate bowl, stirring in a little food color.

2 Place the colored cake batter into a piping bag. Close the bag and snip a tiny triangle off the pointed end.

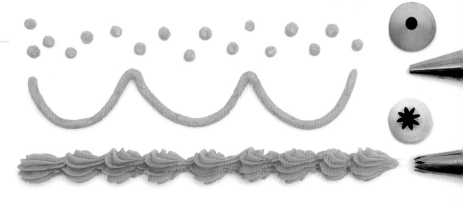

Simple piping techniques

There is nothing mysterious about piping. Squeeze the bag and the icing comes out of the nozzle. Release the pressure and it stops. It's as simple as that. A great place to start is with polka dots, then graduate to loops.

Going dotty

As well as having a contemporary look, piped dots are a great way to detract attention from any blemishes on the cake's surface.

- Use a number 2 or 3 piping nozzle (depending upon how big you want your dots to be) and squeeze a tiny bit of icing out of it, release the pressure, and lift up the nozzle.

Loops

Loops look very elegant and classic on a cake. To help your loops appear the same distance apart you can make a series of marks around the top of the cake to guide you.

- Gently press the piping nozzle against the side of the cake. Squeeze the bag and pull away from the cake. For a second or so you should have a string of icing suspended in midair. It will automatically drop into a loop shape. Move the nozzle back toward the cake and the loop should stick against the cake.

Shells

This is the style of piping often used around the top or base of a cake. You would usually use a star nozzle to create the shells, although a plain version, called a snail trail, can be done using a plain round number 3 nozzle.

- Squeeze a little icing out of the bag, release the pressure and move the bag slightly to the right against the cake, allowing the icing to tail off and thin slightly (move to the left if you're left-handed). Repeat this process all the way around the cake.

Soften the buttercream

For dots, loops, and writing, the buttercream must be very soft. It can help if you add a little water to it to make it not quite runny but softer than the consistency you would use for spreading.

3 Spoon the uncolored batter into cupcake liners and pipe dots of colored batter into it.

4 Bake for about 15 minutes. Try to remove them from the oven when they are springy to the touch but before they start to brown on top.

TRY IT

255 POLKA-DOT CUPCAKES AND CAKE POPS

Piping dots is an easy way to add a little sophistication to a cupcake or some fun to a cake pop. Place a little watered-down buttercream or royal icing in a piping bag with a number 2 piping nozzle and pipe some dots onto your cupcake or cake pop.

Piping animals and faces

You will not need to pipe lots of details to create expressive faces. With just a few candies and a whole heap of enthusiasm you can create a multitude of characters and convey a variety of expressions.

256

Puppy

This adorable little puppy is easy to create. For a darker coat you could make him using chocolate buttercream.

Ingredients
1 tbsp buttercream
3 little bits of black fondant or 3 tiny bits of licorice
1 tiny pink candy
Piping bag with star nozzle attached
Toothpick

1 Place the buttercream into the piping bag and pipe a few vertical lines across the middle of the cupcake.

2 Pipe some squiggly ears, a fringe, and a section across the base of the cupcake for his muzzle.

3 Add two black fondant dots for his eyes, another dot for his nose, and a pink candy for his tongue. "Rough" the buttercream up a little with the toothpick to make his fur a bit more realistic.

257

Candy decorations

Using candies to decorate your buttercream topping is a great alternative to piping. You can create perfectly shaped facial features with the right candy selection.

▶ **Teddy face**
Spread a little chocolate buttercream over the top of the cupcake. Add a marshmallow muzzle, two white chocolate buttons for the eyes, and two milk chocolate buttons for the ears. Stick two chocolate chips onto the eyes with buttercream and another two onto the muzzle for the nose and mouth.

258

Girl

You can have fun creating all sorts of faces with a few candies, cookies, and a food color pen.

Ingredients
1 cookie
1 tbsp buttercream
2 white chocolate buttons
1 red candy string
1 sliced section of red jelly bean
Black food color pen
Piping bag fitted with number 3 piping nozzle

1 Stick the cookie onto the cupcake with a dab of buttercream.

2 Add white chocolate button eyes and a sliced section of red jelly bean. Draw pupils on the eyes with the food color pen.

3 Pipe wiggly hair over the top and sides of the head and finish with a red candy string tied into a bow.

◀ **Caterpillar**

Cover the top of the cupcake with green-colored buttercream. Use a marshmallow for the head and stick alternate milk and white chocolate buttons around the edge of the cupcake to form his body. Place a little buttercream onto his head and add two white buttons for his eyes and half a milk chocolate one for his mouth. Insert two cut sections of red candy string for his feelers and stick a few more sections around the body for his legs. Finish with two black food color dots on his eyes.

▶ **Toadstool**

Take a cupcake out of its wrapper and turn it upside down. Spread red buttercream over the outside of the cupcake and stick it onto a marshmallow. Press a few white chocolate buttons onto the top of the toadstool to finish.

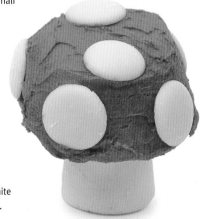

Frozen buttercream transfers

This is a way of transferring a premade frozen design onto a buttercream cake. Your design can be as simple or as complex as you like and involve as many colors as you wish.

► Frozen delights
Frozen transfers aren't limited to just large cakes, they can be used to decorate mini cakes or cupcakes too.

Making a frozen transfer

As its name implies, this technique involves freezing buttercream, therefore you will need a freezer. The advantage of making a frozen decoration is that it can be made well in advance of a party and kept in the freezer until required. The transfers should only be used on cakes covered with buttercream, because the oil from the buttercream transfer can bleed into fondant.

1 Choose a picture or design to use as your template for tracing. One design is given opposite, but you could use an image from a magazine or a book. Tape your design onto a cake card (a thin cake board), place a base sheet of acetate, waxed paper, or plastic wrap over the top, and tape that down securely too.

2 Using a bag fitted with a number 2 piping nozzle, trace around the outline of your design with a dark-colored buttercream.

3 Using different bags with different colors fill in the spaces between the outline. Use a side-to-side motion to fill the different shapes. Place another sheet of acetate, waxed paper, or plastic wrap on top of the iced design and gently smooth over the design with your finger to blend the icing.

4 Place the transfer into the freezer for at least an hour, and then when you are ready to use it remove the top sheet.

5 Carefully lift the base sheet, turn it over, and place the buttercream transfer onto the top of your prepared cake. Carefully remove the remaining sheet of acetate, paper, or plastic wrap. You can decorate further with buttercream piping if you wish.

260

Five rules for designing your transfer

- Don't make your design too intricate since the lines will simply bleed together.

- If you are using a number or letter remember to flip it when you're tracing it so that the number is the right way round when you place it on the cake.

- Don't leave the piped outlines exposed for too long before filling them. They will begin to air dry and will snap and move when you start to fill them.

- If you are making a celebration cake try linking the colors in your design to the color scheme of your party.

- Don't assume you need to use loads of colors. Limiting your design to three or four can be just as striking.

TRY IT

261 LETTERING
The frozen transfer technique will work for lettering as well as for pictures. A dramatically designed initial or number can make a good design for a cake. You can also use transfers on buttercream cupcakes.

FIX IT

262 AIR BUBBLES
If you are using plastic wrap and you find an air bubble developing, prick it with a pin.

▼ **Transfer template**
Trace the flower and petals below onto a piece of cardstock to serve as a template for your own buttercream transfer.

263

Perfect corners

If you can't quite get the buttercream into an awkward corner you can use the tip of a soft paintbrush to gently ease it in there.

Buttercream flowers

Buttercream flowers are very versatile and can be used to decorate cakes for many different celebrations. As with other piped buttercream techniques, all these flowers can also be made with royal icing. As a general rule you should only put buttercream flowers onto a buttercreamed cake and royal iced flowers on a fondant-covered cake.

▲ Frosting flowers
When making flowers always make a few extra and keep them in the freezer. You never know when you might need them!

Professional kit: piping nail

This is a simple piece of equipment that looks, as its name suggests, like a huge nail. Using one allows you to pipe with one hand while gently rotating the nail with the other.

FIX IT

 NO PIPING NAIL?
If you don't have a piping nail you can make your own by sticking a skewer into an aluminum foil-covered cork or taping a drinking straw to an aluminum foil-covered piece of cardstock.

Using a piping nail

These flowers work well in all sorts of colors. If you pipe each flower onto waxed paper and let them harden in the fridge or freezer for a short time, it is easier to lift and place them into position on the cake with a palette knife without breakages.

1 Stick a small square of waxed paper onto the head of the piping nail. Use a dab of buttercream to hold it in place.

2 Holding the bag so that the nozzle is almost flat, and with the widest part of the nozzle in the center of the flower, squeeze a little icing out. Move the piping nail around at the same time. Release the pressure and squeeze again to form a second petal.

3 Continue all the way round to form a circular flower. Remove the flower from the nail. When the flower is in position on the cake, pipe a dot in the center in a contrasting color to finish.

Dot 'n' dash flower

These simple flowers are created using a plain round piping nozzle. They need to be piped directly onto the cake or a plaque (see page 75).

1 Pipe a colored dot onto the cake for the center of the flower.

2 To pipe a petal, squeeze a little icing out of the bag. Release the pressure and pull the bag away from the center of the flower. The icing should tail off to form a petal shape.

3 Repeat step 2, piping petals all around the flower. Add a few leaves using a leaf nozzle. To pipe a leaf, squeeze a little green-colored buttercream out of the leaf nozzle, release the pressure and pull away. The buttercream will tail away leaving a leaf shape behind.

Star flowers

Using a star nozzle you can create easy flowers that look effective on their own or in groups or chains around the cake.

▼ Flower borders
Even with just these few piped flowers at your disposal you can easily create a pretty floral cake.

1 Squeeze a little icing out of the bag. Release the pressure and gently poke the nozzle back into the star. Lift the nozzle away. The icing should break away leaving a star flower behind.

2 Pipe a dot in a contrasting color in the center or add an edible silver ball.

Hyacinths

You will need both a star nozzle and a plain nozzle to create these colorful spring blooms.

Pipe a straight line for the stem followed by a line of stars on either side of it. Finish by piping a couple of lines for the leaves.

African violets

Color some buttercream purple and using the technique shown on page 122, pipe some purple flowers. Pipe a yellow dot in the center of each flower. Allow to set, then place onto the cupcake and finish with a couple of piped leaves.

Realistic rose

This creates a lovely realistic rose, which with a bit of practice is surprisingly easy to create. You will need a petal nozzle and a piping nail. If you are creating tiny roses, pipe them onto waxed paper squares. If you are creating large roses you will need a large petal nozzle, a large piping nail, and a pair of scissors. You can pipe large roses directly onto the nail.

1 Begin by piping the center of the rose: Holding the bag with the thin end pointing upward, pipe a cone shape turning the nail at the same time.

2 Keep the nozzle in the same position and squeeze a little icing out to form a petal. Twist the nail a little at the same time. Release pressure on the bag and pull away. You should now have a petal. Repeat to pipe a second one.

3 Continue piping petals around the roses building it up to the required size.

4 If you have created a tiny rose on waxed paper, place it in the fridge to harden before placing it onto the cake. If you have made a large rose you should be able to lift it using a clean pair of scissors and place it into position on the cake. Splay the scissors open and, holding them horizontally, slide them under the rose. Lift and place the rose directly onto the cake.

 272

Hydrangeas

Fit a large closed star nozzle into a piping bag. Place a spoonful of blue-colored and a spoonful of purple-colored buttercream into the bag and close it. Starting from the outside of the cake, pipe stars around the outer edge then fill in the center.

 273

Too hot to handle?

If the heat from your hand begins to make the buttercream in your piping bag too soft to hold its shape, place the whole bag into the fridge or freezer for 10 minutes or so.

 274

Rose pops

How about a buttercream rose pop? You will need a large petal nozzle and lollipop sticks to create these.

1 Take a ball of cake-pop mixture and gently squeeze it into a cone shape. Pop it onto a lollipop stick and freeze for about 15 minutes.

2 Holding the piping nozzle vertically, with the widest part of the opening at the base, pipe a central cone around the pop, twisting the stick as you pipe.

275

Rose border

If you want to create a rose border, pipe a small green line for the stalk using a number 2 plain nozzle. Pipe a couple of rosettes onto the stalk. Finish with a couple of leaves using the leaf nozzle.

3 Build up petals around the central cone in the same way as you did for the realistic rose opposite. You may find excess icing gathering on the end of the nozzle, so keep your buttercream bowl handy to wipe it off.

4 Chocolate

Chocolate is made from the seed of the cacao tree and the earliest record of chocolate use is around 1100 BCE. Chocolate and cake have been used together in wonderful ways for centuries, both in cooking and cake decoration. The following pages contain some exciting techniques, designs, and ideas for you to try at home.

Working with chocolate

Chocolate is a popular and versatile flavoring, but not all chocolate is the same. The way it tastes and how it is used depends upon a number of factors, including the amount of cocoa butter—the fat that provides that melt-in-your-mouth quality—and cocoa solids (cocoa powder) it contains.

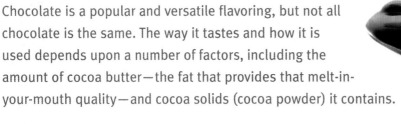

 276

Common types of chocolate

As a general rule the higher the percentage of cocoa solids the better quality the chocolate, but because even cheap brands generally contain relatively high amounts of cocoa solids, plain chocolate can be used successfully in most baking.

TYPE OF CHOCOLATE	GENERAL DESCRIPTION	USES	TYPE OF COCOA
PLAIN CHOCOLATE	This is a popular, slightly bitter tasting confectionery chocolate.	Popular for baking and creating chocolate decorations and desserts.	Contains between 30 and 70 percent cocoa solids.
MILK CHOCOLATE	This is probably the world's favorite type of eating chocolate.	Less popular for baking recipes, but still very useful for decorations and designs.	It has a lower percentage of cocoa solids than dark chocolate, which gives it a less intense flavor.
WHITE CHOCOLATE	Creamy white in color, white chocolate has a much sweeter taste than darker brands and can be used for both eating and cooking.	Despite its lack of cocoa, it can still be melted and used to create all sorts of wonderful designs and sweet treats.	Technically, white chocolate shouldn't really be called chocolate at all, since it contains no cocoa solids. Some white chocolate brands don't even contain any cocoa butter either and use vegetable oils instead.
COUVERTURE	Popular chocolate choice for serious chefs because it has a strong flavor and produces chocolate with a wonderful glossy finish; however, it is quite costly.	Couverture usually needs to be precisely tempered (see page 130), so always read the packaging instructions before using. You will normally have to grate or chop couverture into equal-sized chunks before using to help it melt evenly.	Couverture contains an extremely high percentage of cocoa butter (between 32 and 39 percent).
CHOCOLATE CHIPS, BUTTONS, OR COINS	They are available from chocolate sellers in plain, milk, white, and even flavored varieties.	Because these little button-sized chips of couverture are all the same size they melt evenly, which makes them ideal for tempering.	As these are usually made of couverture, they have a high percentage of cocoa butter.
CHOCOLATE-FLAVORED CAKE COVERINGS	Cooking chocolate, as it is often called, can usually be found in the "home baking" section of the supermarket.	It is popular and melts easily because it has a very high fat content. If you feel that it does not taste as chocolaty as "proper" chocolate, mix a few squares of plain chocolate in with the cooking chocolate while you're melting it to improve the flavor. It is usually available in plain, milk, and white versions and is probably the easiest (and usually cheapest) type of chocolate to experiment with.	These tend to have a high fat content and often no cocoa at all, but a chocolate flavor that is added instead.
COCOA	Concentrated powder that is produced when all the cocoa butter is extracted from chocolate.	It has a strong taste that makes it ideal for flavoring cakes, buttercream, drinks, and even marzipan.	A strong unsweetened chocolate powder.

277

Storing chocolate

Chocolate begins to melt at around body temperature (98°F/37°C). You will need to ensure that your chocolate is stored in a cool, dry place, ideally at a temperature somewhere between 60°F and 64°F (16°C and 18°C). Keep it in its wrapper until required.

278

Beware of water

On the whole, chocolate and water do not mix, so you must be careful when melting chocolate not to get any water in it. If you do, the chocolate will become gritty. This is called seizing. Once your chocolate has seized you will not be able to re-melt it and regain a smooth consistency. For that reason, be careful about using a recently washed wooden spoon for stirring your chocolate in case it is still a little bit damp.

279

Melting chocolate

Unless you are a professional chocolatier, who has a special machine for both melting and tempering your chocolate, you will probably use a heatproof bowl to melt chocolate in. There are two methods for doing this, and in both cases you need to make sure your bowl is sparkling clean and completely dry before you start.

Using a microwave
Break the chocolate into equal-sized pieces and place into the bowl. Heat for 15 seconds or so in an 800–1,000 watt microwave. Check it and microwave again. Stir occasionally. Chocolate will burn if it overheats, so it is best to keep checking every few seconds or so.

Using a stovetop
You cannot melt chocolate over direct heat, so break the chocolate into equal-sized chunks and place into a heatproof bowl. Sit the bowl over a pan of gently simmering water on the stovetop. The bottom of the bowl should not touch the water. Stir occasionally, but make sure that you don't get any water or condensation from the steam in the chocolate because it will seize and become gritty and unusable.

▶ **Weighing it up**
At around 540 calories per 4 oz (125 g) you should go easy on the chocolate portion sizes!

▶ **Cocoa powder**
Cocoa contains various minerals: calcium, magnesium, and sodium. You could almost say it's a healthy option!

280

Tempering chocolate

Tempering involves heating and cooling the chocolate while keeping a close check on its temperature at all times to avoid different-sized crystals from forming. If this happens, the chocolate may "bloom" or become crumbly. If the chocolate is tempered correctly it will contain only small crystals, producing chocolate that has a shiny gloss finish and makes a satisfactory snap when broken. It is especially important to temper the chocolate if you are using couverture or another chocolate with a high cocoa butter content, particularly if you are producing chocolate decorations. Tempering confectionery chocolate will reduce the likelihood of it blooming, but it will not have the polished shine of couverture. It will still taste good though!

If you are melting confectionery or cooking chocolate for use in a baking recipe, or for chocolate rice krispies squares or cake pops, it is not necessary to temper the chocolate first.

There are various ways to temper your chocolate. You will need a thermometer for all of them. If you are not using chocolate chips, either grate or chop the chocolate into equal-sized chunks first to help achieve even melting.

Traditional marble slab method

Although any cool surface will do, marble is traditionally used for tempering chocolate because it provides a cool, natural surface to help bring the temperature of the chocolate down.

1 Melt the chocolate very, very gently in a bowl over a pan of simmering water. The bowl should not touch the water. Stir as you melt it to distribute the heat evenly. The temperature should never exceed 104°F–113°F (40°C–45°C). Once melted, pour about two-thirds of it onto the marble slab.

2 Using the scraper, work the chocolate back and forth across the marble until you can feel it beginning to thicken. Take the temperature. It needs to be down to 82°F (28°C).

3 Scrape the cooled chocolate off the marble and put it back into the original bowl. Stir it into the remaining chocolate and take the temperature again. Plain chocolate needs to be 88°F–90°F (31°C–32°C), milk chocolate 86°F–88°F (30°C–31°C), and white chocolate 80°F–82°F (27°C–28°C). You may need to gently heat the chocolate up a little. Once it has reached the correct temperature it is ready to use.

FIX IT

281 CHOCOLATE STILL TOO WARM?
If, when you return the chocolate to the original bowl it is still too warm, tip a little out, work it on the marble slab again until it begins to thicken and return it to the bowl. Stir and take the temperature again. Repeat until the required temperature is reached.

Bowl and water method

This method may take a bit of time but it's worth it. The chocolate must be melted very slowly, and it may also take a while for it to cool down to the correct temperature at the end stage.

You will need
Heatproof bowl
Saucepan with about 2 in (5 cm) of simmering water in it
Metal spoon
Thermometer
Towel

Melting in the microwave

If you don't want to use the stovetop for melting your chocolate you can use a microwave. Grate or break the chocolate into a bowl and heat it for about 15 seconds, check it, and repeat. Continue until the chocolate has almost melted and then remove from the microwave. Stir in the remaining chocolate. Check the temperature as outlined in step 3 of the traditional marble slap method, opposite.

1 Grate or break the chocolate up into even-sized chunks and gently melt about two-thirds of it in the bowl over the saucepan of water, stirring occasionally. The bowl should not be touching the water. When the chocolate has melted, take the bowl off and wrap the towel around the base of the bowl to keep the chocolate warm.

2 Put the leftover chocolate into the bowl and stir it in. It should melt and mix together. Use a thermometer to check the temperature. Plain chocolate needs to be 88°F–90°F (31°C–32°C), milk chocolate 86°F–88°F (30°C–31°C), and white chocolate 80°F–82°F (27°C–28°C). When the mixture has reached the correct temperature for its type it is ready to use.

Blooming chocolate

Sometimes you might see whitish patches of bloom on your chocolate. Usually this is caused by the chocolate being stored in slightly damp conditions. It can also happen if you have tempered the chocolate on too high a heat, causing the cocoa fat to separate and come to the surface of the chocolate. Although it doesn't look great it is still perfectly safe to eat chocolate that has bloomed.

FIX IT

284 NO MARBLE SLAB?
You can still temper your chocolate successfully even if you don't have a marble slab. Simply use the back of a cookie sheet, which will cool your chocolate down equally well.

◄ **Feeling fruity**
Fresh fruit can be used to create attractive decorations for chocolate-covered cakes.

Ganache

Ganache is a mixture of rich, dark chocolate and cream. Although indulgent and insanely calorific, it's an extremely versatile chocolate recipe that has many uses. It can be poured over the top of a cake or whipped and used as a thick chocolaty filling and covering.

▲ **Lovely and luscious**
Ganache makes a fantastic topping for chocolate cake.

285

Ganache recipe

There are many recipes for ganache. Here is one of the simplest for an 8 in (20 cm) diameter round chocolate cake. You do not need to temper the chocolate first.

You will need
8 oz (250 g) good quality dark
    chocolate
8 fl oz (250 ml) double cream
Grater
Heatproof bowl
Saucepan
Whisk (handheld or electric)

1 Grate or break the chocolate into even-sized pieces and place it into the bowl. Gently heat the cream in the saucepan until it simmers.

FIX IT

286 SEPARATED GANACHE
Occasionally, when you pour the cream over the chocolate you may find that the ganache separates and becomes a grainy mixture, with what looks like oil floating on the top.

To stop this from happening, the chocolate and cream need to be similar temperatures. The chocolate should be warm and at room temperature, not straight from the refrigerator or a cold room/cellar. Pour the simmering cream over the chocolate and let it sit for 10 minutes before whisking.

You can save separated ganache if you have a food processor or a handheld electric blender. Place the separated ganache into the food processor with 2 tbsp (30 ml) of cream and mix it until it comes back together.

2 Pour the simmering cream onto the chocolate and allow it to sit for 10 minutes, stirring occasionally.

3 Whisk until the mixture is smooth. Allow it to cool slightly. At this smooth, runny stage the ganache can be poured over your cake.

4 If you want a spreadable covering and/or filling, let the mixture cool down. It should thicken as it does so. Once it's cooled, whisk until light and fluffy.

287

Covering your cake

Some bakers like to cover the cake with some chocolate marzipan first for a smooth finish. This will provide a perfect surface for the ganache to adhere to.

You will need
8 in (20 cm) diameter round chocolate cake, split and
    filled with chocolate buttercream or thick whipped
    chocolate ganache
1 lb 2 oz (500 g) marzipan
2–3 tbsp (30–45 ml) cocoa powder
3 tbsp (45 ml) apricot jam
1 quantity thick, runny ganache (see opposite)
Palette knife
Rolling pin
Cake smoother (optional)
Spatula for lifting cake
Cake board or plate

1 Knead about 2 tbsp (30 ml) of cocoa powder into the marzipan. It should turn a rich, even chocolate brown color.

2 Spread the apricot jam over the top and sides of the cake.

3 Roll out the marzipan, lift it, and place it on top of the cake.

4 Smooth the top and sides and cut away any unwanted marzipan from around the base of the cake.

5 Using the spatula, to try and prevent too many fingerprints, lift and place the cake on a plate or cake board.

6 Mix up the ganache and pour it over the cake. Using the palette knife, ease it over the top and sides.

288

Ganache on a small scale

Ganache works as a topping for small cakes, too. These cupcakes are baked using the two-egg pound cake recipe (see page 16). Two tbsp (30 ml) of cocoa powder and a handful of chocolate chips are stirred into the mix before baking.

Use a piping bag fitted with a star nozzle, filled with ganache to pipe a swirl on the top of each cupcake. Complete your cupackes with edible gold balls or stars.

You will need
12 chocolate cupcakes already
    baked in cupcake liners
1 quantity of ganache, cooled and
    whipped to a piping consistency
    (see opposite)
Edible gold balls, stars, or similar
    to decorate
Piping bag
Large star nozzle
Spatula

TRY IT

289   SPICE IT UP
If you want to add an extra kick to your ganache, add 1 tbsp (15 ml) of rum or another flavored liquor to the mixture once it has cooled.

▶ **Cake stands**
Cake stands can really help to elevate your cupcakes' status on the tea table!

Decorating with chocolate

Chocolate can be used to create a variety of decorations for your cakes, and many are much easier to produce than you might think. You can make some beautiful molded chocolate pieces that will bring sophistication to any sweet treat.

Chocolate leaves

Chocolate leaves are a delicate way to add a special finish to your cakes. Rose leaves work well, as do holly leaves—just be careful not to prick yourself! It's a good idea to make more leaves than you think you might need in case some break when you're peeling them off.

The leaves need to be pesticide free, and rinsed and dried thoroughly with a paper towel to remove any moisture.

1 Hold the leaf by the stem and gently dip one side only into the melted chocolate. Spread with a paintbrush. Dipping the underside of the leaf will produce the best, veined results.

2 Repeat, making as many leaves as you require. Place them onto a baking sheet and refrigerate for about 5 minutes until they feel firm but not completely hard.

FIX IT

291 MISSHAPEN DECORATION?
If something goes wrong with your chocolate decoration, then as long as it's not burned and has not seized, you can always pop it back into the bowl, remelt it, and start again.

3 Carefully peel the chocolate away and discard the real leaf.

Chocolate shavings

You'll need to rummage in your kitchen drawer to find a vegetable peeler to make these. Use these shavings to decorate sumptuous chocolate cakes, desserts, or trifles.

Simply run the peeler along the edge of a block of chocolate to create these artistic edible curls and shavings.

▲ **Chocolate and flowers**
Non-poisonous, food safe-flowers (see page 94 for list) can be crystallized and used as decorations. Nestle them between a few chocolate leaves.

293

Mini chocolate cups

A paper petit-four liner can become a simple chocolate mold. It is best to use a good quality chocolate for this project and temper it before use (see page 130). To make a chocolate cup, use a dry pastry brush to paint a thin coating of melted chocolate around the inside of the petit-four liner. Allow it to set, then carefully peel away the paper liner.

You can use your chocolate cups in many ways—as edible liners for dipped fruits, chocolate candies, or even handmade chocolate truffles (see page 141).

294

White curls

You don't always need to stick to the darker varieties of chocolate, why not mix it up a bit? Use a vegetable peeler to generously shave white chocolate on top of your frosted cupcake. If the chocolate gets too warm, pop it into the refrigerator for a couple of minutes to firm up.

FIX IT

297 CURLS CRACKING?
To stop the curls from cracking, the chocolate should be room temperature not straight out of the refrigerator. It also helps if you use chocolate with a low cocoa butter content.

295

Positioning your chocolate decorations

Decorations such as curls or shavings can simply be sprinkled onto the cake, but if you want to stick something into a certain position—a cluster of leaves or chocolate shapes for example—then "glue" them in place with little dabs of melted chocolate.

296

Chocolate-dipped fruits

You can dip all sorts of fruit into chocolate, including strawberries, orange segments, and grapes. Although they won't keep for a long time, they are fun and could be used as cake or dessert decorations.

Take your chosen fruit and dip it into melted chocolate. Place the dipped fruit onto a sheet of parchment paper to set.

If you want to take this concept further you could pop your dipped fruits onto sticks to create dipped-fruit chocolate lollipops. You could also add a few sprinkles if you wish. These would make a fun addition to any birthday party.

▲ **Chocolate delight**
Here chocolate transfers and leaves have been used to create an elegant chocolate wedding confection.

298

Making chocolate shapes

It is perfectly possible to cut shapes out of chocolate but it must be done before the chocolate has set too firmly. The trick is not to melt too much chocolate at one time. By working on a small scale you don't run the risk of the chcolate hardening before you have cut out your shapes. Use good-quality chocolate and temper it before cutting into it (see page 130). You can use a sharp knife, decorative cutters, or even a pizza wheel for cutting out different shapes.

Place a sheet of parchment paper on a baking sheet. Melt and temper the chocolate and, using a spatula, spread it over the parchment paper to a thickness of about ⅛ in (3 mm). Place it in the refrigerator for approximately 5 minutes. The chocolate should be cool and firm but not completely rock hard and solid.

Using a cutter
Press the cutter into the chocolate and cut out your shape. Although you can use any cutter, metal cutters tend to produce a cleaner cut than plastic ones. They should be clean, dry, and at room temperature. Place the shapes onto a separate sheet of parchment paper until they are required.

Using a sharp knife
The knife should be nonserrated, sharp, and clean. Slice it through the chocolate and cut out your chosen shape. Carefully remove them from the original baking sheet and place onto a second one to set completely.

Using a pizza cutter
Use the pizza cutter to carefully slice through the chocolate. When cut, remove from the first baking sheet and place onto a second sheet to firm up before use. A pizza cutter is especially useful for creating long rectangular strips.

Chocolate medals
Cut out some chocolate disks and make a hole in the top of each one with a small circle cutter or drinking straw. When hardened, pipe a number 1 on each medal and thread onto a little ribbon.

Chocolate people
Use a gingerbread man cutter to cut out some chocolate people and decorate with a few chocolate chips or piped melted chocolate.

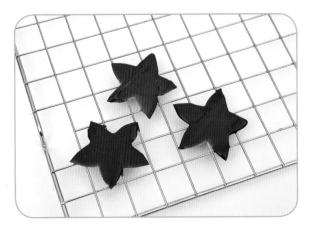

299

Edible wafer paper shapes

Another way of making chocolate shapes is to use a sheet of edible wafer paper (rice paper). Cut the paper into the required shape then dip one side into melted chocolate. Allow it to dry on a cooling rack or sheet of parchment paper, then use as required. Because it is edible, you do not have to remove the wafer paper before serving. If the chocolate has overrun the edges slightly you may find you need to slice off the excess with a sharp, nonserrated knife to clean the shape up.

300

Chocolate transfer sheets

This is both an easy and very pretty way to decorate your chocolate shapes. Chocolate transfer sheets are readily available from cake decorating stores and the Internet, and come in a huge range of patterns including spots, stripes, animal prints, flowers, and even regency swirls!

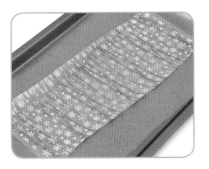

1 Place a sheet of parchment paper on a baking sheet and place the transfer, shiny side downward, on the parchment paper.

2 Melt and temper the chocolate and, using a spatula, spread it over the transfer sheet to a thickness of about ⅛ in (3 mm). Place it in the fridge for approximately 5 minutes. The chocolate should be cool and firm but not completely rock hard and solid.

FIX IT

301 WHAT TO DO WITH TRANSFER MISTAKES

If you are using plain or milk chocolate and your transfers don't go according to plan, don't waste the chocolate. Simply remelt it and start again. The transfer coloring will not be visible once it is mixed into the melted chocolate. Similarly, you can reuse offcuts and remelt the chocolate for a new use.

3 Cut out your desired shapes using a cutter or a knife, then leave to set completely.

4 Once the chocolate has set, peel away the transfer paper. Your decorated shapes are now ready for use.

302

Chocolate lace bowl

This little bowl, together with a couple of homemade—or store-bought if you're in a rush—truffles, would make a lovely, delicate gift for someone special. The bigger the bowl, the more chocolate you will need. As a rough guide, a 29 fl oz (850 ml) pudding bowl would need about 8 oz (250 g) of chocolate. The small bowl shown here only required 3½ oz (100 g) of chocolate; however, it depends on how dense you want your lace to be—the thicker the chocolate piping, the stronger the bowl. You could use a combination of milk, white, and plain chocolate.

1 Line a bowl with plastic wrap. Smooth it down so that there are no trapped pockets of air. Allow the excess plastic wrap to hang over the side of the bowl. It will help you to release the chocolate bowl later.

2 Melt and temper your chocolate (see page 130) and place it into a piping bag. Snip a tiny triangle off of the end and pipe around the inside of the bowl. The lines can be as wiggly as you want and can go in all directions. Repeat using more chocolate as necessary.

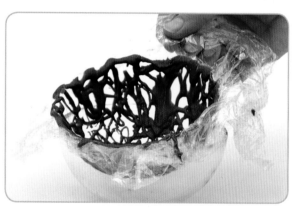

3 Leave the bowl to set. When the chocolate has hardened, pull the wrap to gently ease it out of the bowl. You may find a small palette knife is useful for loosening any particularly stubborn bits.

303

Chocolate squiggles

As the name suggests, these are simply squiggles of melted chocolate. They are easy to make and will add a bit of fun to any cake or dessert.

Place some tempered chocolate into a piping bag and snip the end off. The larger the opening, the wider your squiggles will be. Pipe some squiggly lines onto parchment paper and allow them to harden before use.

If you don't have a piping bag you could just drizzle a wiggly chocolate line onto a sheet of parchment paper using a teaspoon.

FIX IT

304
BROKEN CHOCOLATE BOWL
If a chunk breaks off of your chocolate bowl, stick it back together with a little melted chocolate. If the whole lot breaks, simply remelt and start again.

◄ Magical molds
Mold designs can be intricate like these fish or simple like the hearts.

305

Molded chocolate decorations

Once you start looking for chocolate molds you will find an incredible array of designs available, usually made in flexible plastic. Available from kitchen and cake decorating stores and online, they are not particularly expensive either. The golden rule is that the mold must be clean and dry before use.

1 For the best results temper your chocolate first and carefully spoon the melted chocolate into the molds. Try to keep the top of the chocolate level with the top of the mold. If it overflows, scrape away the excess.

2 Once they are filled, tap the molds on your work surface to release any air bubbles, which could cause the chocolate to crack, then place into the fridge until the chocolate has hardened. This should take about 10–20 minutes depending on the thickness of the chocolate.

3 When they have set, tip the chocolates out of the molds and hand them around to all your friends, or use for decorations!

306

Piping with chocolate

You can both pipe designs and write messages using chocolate. Simply melt a little chocolate in a heatproof bowl and place into a small piping bag. Fold over the end of the piping bag to close it and snip a little triangle off the end. Carefully squeeze the bag and pipe your design or message onto the cake. Should the chocolate in the bag start to harden you can pop it into the microwave for a few seconds to remelt it.

TRY IT

307 GLOSSY TREATS
Polish your molds with a cotton ball or soft cloth before each application of chocolate to make shiny chocolates.

► Get piping
Designs can be piped and messages written using chocolate.

Chocolate cake pops and truffles

These little treats are easier to make than you might think. Placed in a pretty box, truffles make a delightful gift, and if you want to give cake pops as favors, you can cover them with cake-pop wrappers. Treat cake pops and truffles as you would cake, and eat them within two to three days.

Chocolate cake pops

Chocolate cake pops are not only easy to make, but they taste really good too. They are also useful for using up odd bits of leftover cake.

You will need the same weight of cake crumb as chocolate, so if you have 4 oz (120 g) of cake, use 4 oz (120 g) of chocolate. You can use any type of chocolate—plain, milk, or white—and any type of cake—plain pound, chocolate, or fruit. The pound cake and white chocolate combination is particularly good!

1 Weigh and crumble the cake into a large bowl. Weigh and melt the same amount of chocolate. Melt an additional four squares of chocolate for use with the sticks later.

2 Stir the first batch of chocolate into the cake crumb. Once it has mixed to form a sort of dough, take a small handful and roll it into a ball shape.

3 Take a lollipop stick and dip the tip into the melted chocolate, then poke the chocolate-dipped end into the ball. As it sets, the melted chocolate will help "glue" the pop in place.

4 Stand the cake pop on a baking sheet. If you don't mind a flat bottom, stand them stick upward. If you prefer your pops rounded, you can stand them in a sturdy glass, polystyrene block, or colander while they set. Repeat, making as many pops as you want.

5 Place the pops in the fridge for about an hour, or the freezer for about 15 minutes, to harden. You can leave the pops like this or you can melt more chocolate and dip them in it. You can add chocolate sprinkles and other decorations if you like.

309

Truly tempting chocolate cream truffles

The secret to these sensuous, melt-in-your-mouth truffles is not cake but the ever-versatile ganache.

1 To make your truffles, mix up a batch of ganache following the recipe on page 132. You can use dark, milk, or white chocolate. Once the cream and chocolate have been melted and whisked together, leave the mixture in its bowl to cool down completely. Then cover the bowl and place it in the refrigerator for an hour or so until it feels firm. Using a melon baller or teaspoon, scoop up a ball of ganache.

2 Roll the mixture in your hands to get a nice spherical shape.

3 Sprinkle some cocoa powder into a saucer and roll your truffles in it. Repeat, making as many truffles as you can. Chill them on a baking sheet in the refrigerator for at least an hour before serving.

◀ **Box of delights**
Place a few truffles in a pretty box to make a delightful gift.

TRY IT

310 ALTERNATIVE CAKE-POP BALLS
If you don't have any lollipop sticks, place cake-pop balls in petit-four liners or simply display them on a plate. They taste so delicious they won't hang around for long, with or without a lollipop stick!

311 LEFTOVER CAKE?
Save and freeze the bits of cake that you cut off when leveling a cake so that you can rustle up a batch of pops when needed, and you don't waste any odd bits of cake either.

312

Decorated ganache truffles

You can decorate truffles with chocolate sprinkles while the chocolate is still wet, or pipe chocolate squiggles onto your dipped truffles once the outer coating has set. Always temper the covering chocolate first.

Another pretty way to decorate truffles is to use chocolate transfers (see page 137).

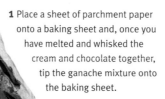

1 Place a sheet of parchment paper onto a baking sheet and, once you have melted and whisked the cream and chocolate together, tip the ganache mixture onto the baking sheet.

2 Spread it out using a spatula and allow the truffle mixture to set. It can be left overnight if you wish.

3 If you have stored the ganache in the refrigerator, allow the mixture to sit out for an hour or so to bring it up to room temperature before you decorate. Slice the sheet of ganache into squares.

4 Cut out a section of transfer paper larger than the top of the truffles.

5 Dip the truffles into melted chocolate using a fork and place on a baking sheet.

6 Gently place the textured side of the transfer onto the wet chocolate and softly press it on top. Leave the transfer paper in place until the chocolate has completely set hard. This could be a couple of hours in the refrigerator or overnight in a cool room.

7 Once the chocolate is set, remove the paper to reveal your truffle in all its glory!

Making your own gift boxes using free templates

Delightful chocolaty truffles demand a special kind of packaging. There are an abundance of websites out there offering free downloadable templates for making every type of box: from heart-shaped ones to cute little boxes with integral lids and handle. Or, if you are looking for something simpler, and quicker, why not cover an existing box with pretty wrapping paper? If you are making a box from scratch a standard piece of cardstock is sufficient for holding truffles. Use a white glue or a craft glue. A template for a simple box is shown here. Simply transfer the template measurements onto your chosen cardstock and cut out with scissors. Fold over all the edges and glue as indicated on the template.

TRY IT

314 DOWNLOAD SOME INSPIRATION
Here are some of the best sites for free box template downloads:

www.mirkwooddesigns.com
Mirkwood Designs have been designing craft templates since 1998 and provide free templates for truffle boxes on www.mirkwooddesigns.com/projects/truffle-boxes.

www.itsalwaysautumn.com
It's Always Autumn provide free template downloads including step-by-step instructions for pretty packaging and tags for tasty treats.

www.designswithheart.net/templates.html
Designs With Heart list ideas for gifts (in jars) or other neat little packages, and paper craft templates and patterns, including a round-topped truffle-box template.

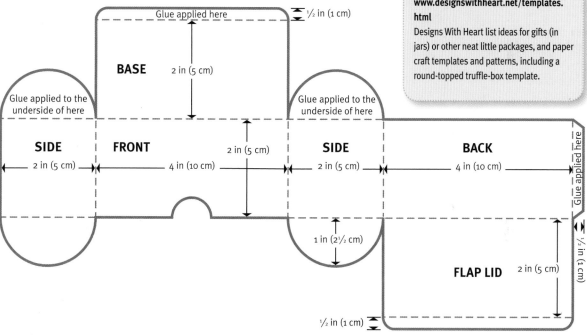

BASE — 2 in (5 cm)
Glue applied here — ½ in (1 cm)
Glue applied to the underside of here
SIDE — 2 in (5 cm) — FRONT — 4 in (10 cm) — 2 in (5 cm) — SIDE — 2 in (5 cm) — BACK — 4 in (10 cm)
Glue applied to the underside of here
Glue applied here
2 in (5 cm)
1 in (2½ cm)
FLAP LID — 2 in (5 cm) — ½ in (1 cm)
½ in (1 cm)

Storing your ganache truffles

Fresh cream truffles should be kept in the refrigerator and eaten within 3 to 4 days. Alternatively, you can freeze them for up to 2 months. Chocolate-coated ganache truffles should be stored in the fridge for 3 to 4 days and can't be frozen.

Clearing up chocolate

Be careful when washing a bowl containing melted chocolate. Be sure to scrape out as much chocolate as you can. Although it's tempting to wash a bowl in hot water, once that chocolate goes down the drain it will cool and solidify and could cause a blockage.

How to make and use templates

Each design in this section is presented as a template on a grid to enable you to resize it easily. If you like a motif design but need to change the dimensions to suit your cake, there are easy ways of doing this. A template can be made for an individual motif, or for the whole cake top.

Paired motifs

Many of the motifs in this section would look good as a pair, facing in opposite directions. They could be used to frame a message, for example. To do this, you can either scan the template and use imaging software to flip it, or trace the motif over a lightbox (see below) and turn the paper over.

Using a grid

This is a straightforward method for scaling your design up to the desired size for your cake.

1 On a sheet of white paper, draw a square or rectangle the size you want the finished motif to be. Use a ruler to divide this box into squares — the number of squares should match those in the original grid.

2 Recreate the original image by replicating the lines that appear in each grid box on the template on your grid. Work square by square until the design has been completely transferred.

The completed motif is shown alongside the template used to create it.

Resizing your grid

You can resize your image using a variety of different methods.

Using a photocopier
Work out the enlargement or reduction in terms of a percentage. For example, if the size of the original picture is 100 percent and you want it twice as big, set the photocopier at 200 percent.

Using a scanner
If you have access to a computer with a scanner, scan the template and use image software to adjust the size of the template to your requirements.

Using a lightbox
A lightbox can be useful to trace a motif to make several copies, or to reverse a motif by flipping it.

320

Using a template

Once you have made the template, put it in a plastic sleeve to protect it. The pattern of the motif can be built up on top of the plastic sleeve and then moved to the top of the cake using a palette knife.

Build up the motif, starting with the bigger, main pieces, and then moving on to the detail. Where colored sections are the same, it is a good idea to work on all these pieces together, which will both save time and prevent colors cross-mixing on the work surface.

The finished motif, ready for transfer to the cake.

1 Use your finger to smear a little vegetable shortening over the template in the plastic sleeve. This will help to keep the components in place as you work on them, but also enable you to remove them easily to transfer the finished motif to the cake.

2 Working from the back of the design, shape the main body elements. Roll a ball and then flatten it into the shape of the template, leaving a bulge in the center of the fondant and smoothing out the edges to fit within the lines.

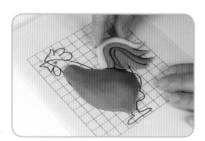

3 Still working with the back components, roll and shape the next section of detail.

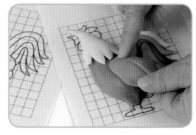

4 Moving toward the front of the design, continue adding the components.

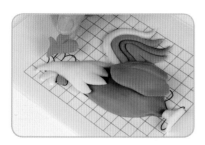

5 Finally, work on the small details, including any marks or textures mentioned in the detailed instructions.

6 Carefully brush on luster where appropriate. If a denser coating of luster is required, brush over the areas with a very small amount of vegetable shortening. This provides a surface that will hold the luster better.

TRY IT

321 TEMPLATE PORTFOLIO

Build up a file of templates so that the designs you use regularly are quickly available when needed. Make a note of the colors and quantities used for your design, so that a quick reference guide is instantly on hand. It is sometimes useful to have two copies of the template — one to work on and the other as a guide to making the components.

322 WORKING AHEAD OF TIME

Motifs can be made and stored in advance of the event for which they are intended. Keep them in a storage container and lift them on the tip of a palette knife to transfer them to the cake. Don't worry about moving the whole motif all at once; it may be easier to transfer the components in several parts. As they have all been molded together originally they will fit closely against one another when reassembled. A very small amount of water brushed onto the back surface will be sufficient to attach them into position.

Topper directory

Pick out your favorite design and follow the instructions beside each one and on pages 144–145 to make up your own cake topper. Color suggestions are provided, but they are only there as guidance, feel free to experiment with your own color ideas.

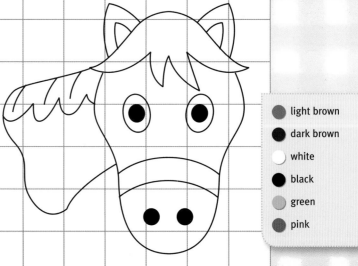

▶ Bird

Shape the lime-green body from a teardrop pressed down onto the template. Add the beak and eye with colored fondant. Shape the tail from a petal shape, and indent it twice. Make the wing from a squashed bulb shape and indent the feathers. Pipe the legs or use strips of licorice.

| lime green |
| blue |
| black |
| white |

▶ Pony head

Use the template to shape the neck; add the mane. Shape the head and add triangular ears and hair. Indent the eyes and nose and insert colored fondant. Twist two pieces of colored fondant together to make a bridle.

| light brown |
| dark brown |
| white |
| black |
| green |
| pink |

► Owl

Smooth a light-brown disk onto the template for the body. Add an orange heart-shaped chest and two pale heart-shaped wings. Create the eyes with layers of fondant following the picture. Add the beak and claws in dark brown. You could perch him on a branch!

- light brown
- orange
- soft orange
- white
- lemon yellow
- dark brown
- black

► Dog

Mold this in two separate parts. First, the body, legs, and tail, adding deeper parts and thinner parts as shown. Mold the head and ears. Indent and add eyes and nose. Place both parts together and cover join with a black collar.

- light brown
- black
- dark brown
- white

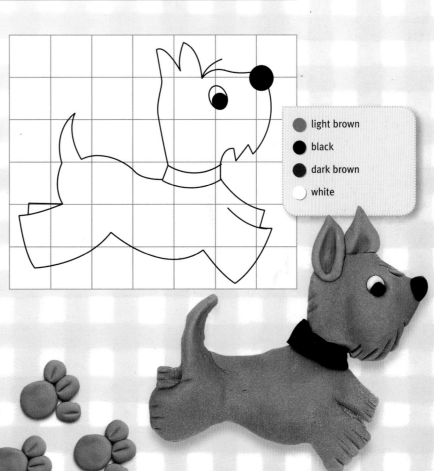

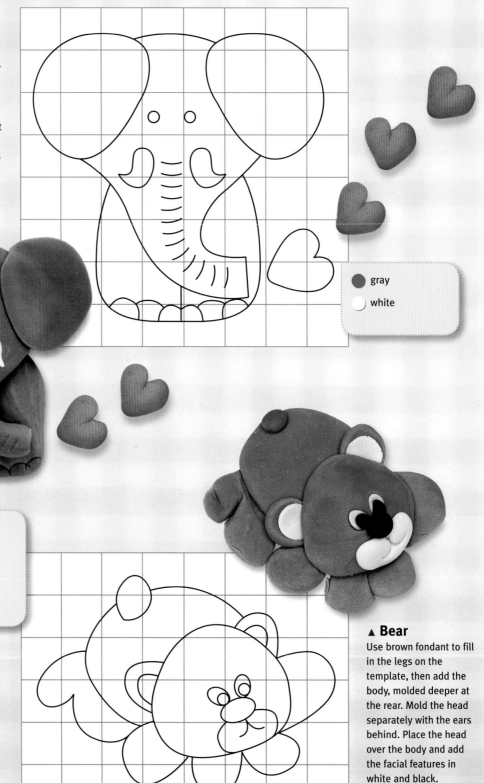

▶ Elephant

Spread gray fondant over the template for the legs and indent the toes with a drinking straw. Shape gray fondant into a carrot shape for the trunk and head. Add flattened balls of fondant for the ears and use bent, white fondant cones for the tusks.

- ● gray
- ○ white

- ● light brown
- ○ white
- ● black
- ● dark brown

▲ Bear

Use brown fondant to fill in the legs on the template, then add the body, molded deeper at the rear. Mold the head separately with the ears behind. Place the head over the body and add the facial features in white and black.

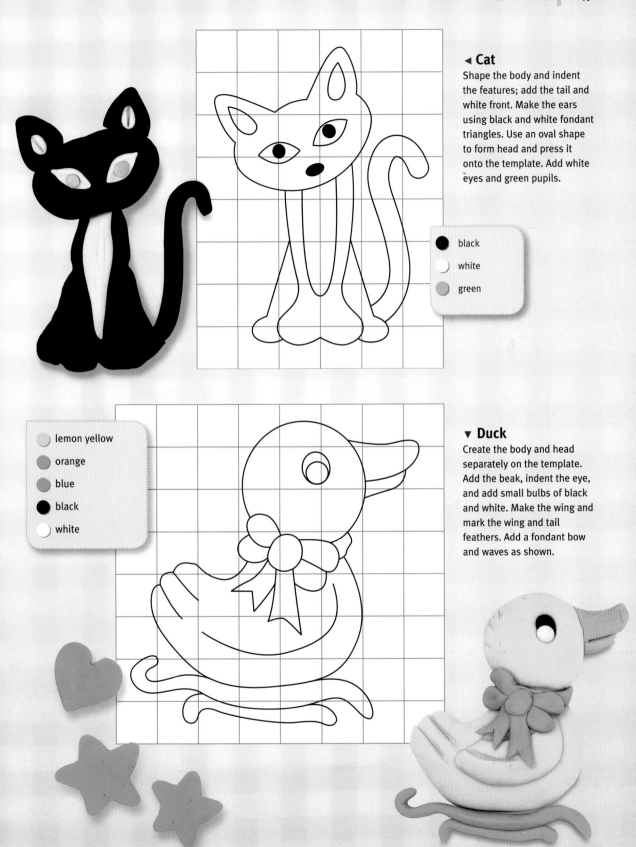

◄ Cat

Shape the body and indent the features; add the tail and white front. Make the ears using black and white fondant triangles. Use an oval shape to form head and press it onto the template. Add white eyes and green pupils.

- ● black
- ○ white
- ● green

▼ Duck

Create the body and head separately on the template. Add the beak, indent the eye, and add small bulbs of black and white. Make the wing and mark the wing and tail feathers. Add a fondant bow and waves as shown.

- ● lemon yellow
- ● orange
- ● blue
- ● black
- ○ white

▲ Poinsettia

Create and indent four green leaves using the template. Add four large and two smaller red petals, add the markings. Flip up the tips of the petals and support them until they're dry. Place small lemon-yellow balls in center to complete.

red

green

lemon yellow

◄ Flower spray

Press five orange teardrop shapes onto template and indent through middle, repeat with smaller teardrops, and fix. Press ball of fondant into the center and mark with small dots. Add three green fondant leaves to fit just beneath petals, mark leaf edges, and veins.

orange

soft orange

green

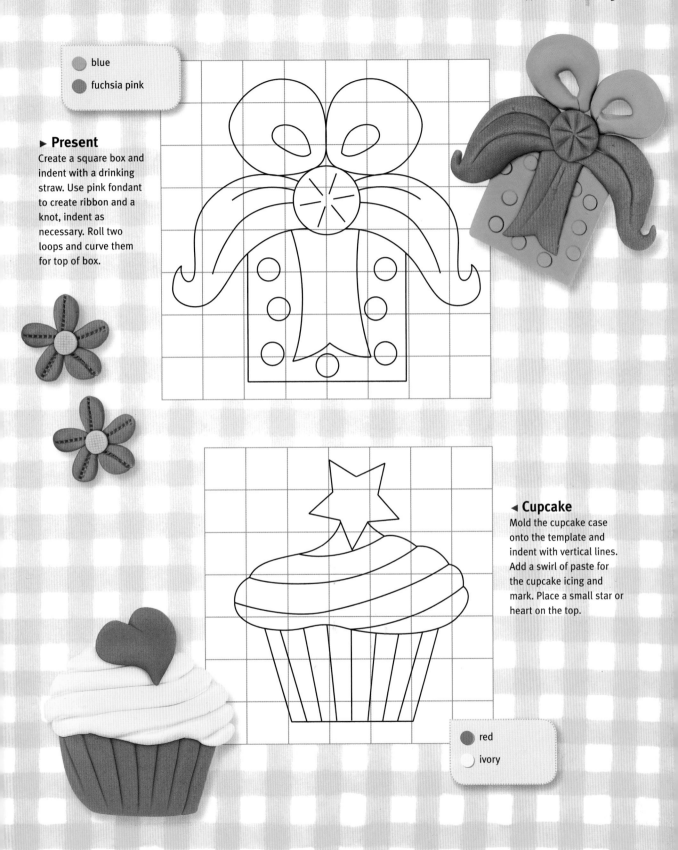

blue

fuchsia pink

▶ Present

Create a square box and indent with a drinking straw. Use pink fondant to create ribbon and a knot, indent as necessary. Roll two loops and curve them for top of box.

◀ Cupcake

Mold the cupcake case onto the template and indent with vertical lines. Add a swirl of paste for the cupcake icing and mark. Place a small star or heart on the top.

red

ivory

▶ Penguin

Shape the black fondant over the triangular template shape. Cut the wings and ease them away from the body. Shape the white front. Indent the eyes with a drinking straw. Finally, shape and add beak and feet.

- ● black
- ○ white
- ● orange

▲ Snowman

Flatten two balls of white fondant on the template for the body and head. Add on the arms. Shape the green scarf, imprint a pattern, and add balls of red. Add two black buttons to the body. Mark the mouth and add the eyes and carrot-shaped nose.

- ○ white
- ● green
- ● red
- ● black
- ● orange

Conversions

You may find you need to convert units of measurement into their metric or imperial equivalents. On these pages the conversions for some common quantities are given.

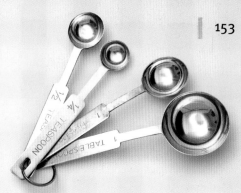

Weight

Imperial	Metric
1 oz	28 g
1 lb	454 g

Metric	Imperial
100 g	3½ oz
1 kg	2¼ lb

Cups	Imperial	Metric
1 cup butter	8 oz	230 g
1 cup brown sugar	7 oz	200 g
1 cup white sugar	6¾ oz	190 g
1 cup chopped pecans	4¼ oz	120 g
1 cup flour	3½ oz	100 g
1 cup ground almonds	3 oz	85 g

Lengths

Imperial	Metric
1 inch	25.4 mm

Metric	Imperial
100 mm	4 inches

Volume

Imperial	Metric
1 fl. oz	30 ml
1 pint (US)	473 ml

Metric	Imperial
100 ml	3½ fl. oz
1 liter (US)	2 pints

Cups	Imperial	Metric
⅛ cup	1 fl. oz	30 ml
1 cup	8 fl. oz	240 ml

Spoon	Imperial	Metric
1 teaspoon	⅙ fl. oz	5 ml
1 dessertspoon	⅓ fl. oz	10 ml
1 tablespoon	½ fl. oz	15 ml

Oven Temperatures

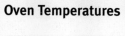

	Fahrenheit	Celsius
Cool	200°	90°
Very slow	250°	120°
Slow	300–325°	150–160°
Moderately slow	325–350°	160–180°
Moderate	350–375°	180–190°
Moderately hot	375–400°	190–200°
Hot	400–450°	200–230°

Glossary

Apricot glaze

Apricot glaze is brushed onto the cake surface to act as a "glue" for the decorative icing layer. An alternative is piping gel.

Blossom cutters

Blossom cutters are used to make small flowers with several petals. Some types incorporate a spring-loaded plunger to eject the flower cleanly once it is cut.

Buttercream icing

Buttercream icing is made from a mixture of butter and confectioners' sugar beaten together, sometimes with meringue powder added to make it smoother. Buttercream icing may be flavored and colored. It may be spread over a cake or used for pipe borders.

Confectioners' sugar

Confectioners' sugar is a very finely ground icing sugar that is used for cake decoration. Sometimes it is labeled "10XXX."

Cornelli work

Cornelli work is a decorative piping technique where lines are piped in curved shapes close to each other to fill in a space.

Cornstarch

Cornstarch (cornflour) is used for dusting the work surface when rolling out fondant and gumpaste.

Crimping

Crimping is a decorative design made by special patterned metal tweezers (crimpers) designed to squeeze the fondant between them.

Edible glue (sugar glue)

Edible glue is used as an adhesive between modeled sugar components.

Embossing

Embossing is the term given to creating a texture on fondant with different tools.

Firm peak

Firm peak describes prepared royal icing when it has been beaten to a firmness where the icing will stay standing up in a peak.

Fondant icing

Fondant icing (sugarpaste) is a soft, pliable paste suitable for covering cakes or modeling. It may be colored and flavored. It is often store-bought and ready-to-roll; alternatively you can make your own.

Gum tragacanth (Gum-Tex)

Gum tragacanth (Gum-Tex) is a hardener used in preparation of gum paste.

Liquid glucose (corn syrup)

Liquid glucose is sometimes used as an ingredient in fondant icing to keep it pliable.

Luster

Luster is used to add color or a shimmering effect to fondant. It can be brushed on.

Meringue powder (albumen powder)

Meringue powder is powdered egg white and is used for making royal icing. Dissolve in water, following the package instructions before use.

Plastic wrap

Plastic wrap is used to wrap cakes to keep them from drying out.

Royal icing

Royal icing is a beaten mixture of egg white and confectioners' sugar suitable for coating cakes and piping. It sets firm and crisp.

Smoothers

Smoothers are flat plastic tools used to smooth over a fondant surface to even out any undulations. Work with two smoothers to achieve the best finish.

Soft peak

Soft peak is a description of prepared royal icing that has softened a little— so that when a peak is pulled up from the surface, the top curves over slightly.

Turntable

A turntable holds a cake during decoration. It revolves so that the top and sides of a cake can be worked on.

Veiner

Veiners are textured silicone, or plastic, tools that are used to press veins into fondant leaves to make them look realistic.

Suppliers

Cake Carousel
1002 N. Central Expessway
Suite 501
Richardson, TX 75080
Tel: 972-690-4628
Or 877-814-6670
www.cakecarousel.com

Wilton
Wilton Industries, Inc
2240 West 75th Street
Woodridge, IL 60517
Tel: 630-963-7100
www.wilton.com

Michaels, The Arts and Crafts Store
Michaels Store Inc.
8000 Bent Branch Dr.
Irving, TX 75063
Tel: 1-800-642-4235
www.michaels.com

Sugarcraft, Inc
3665 Dixie Hwy
Hamilton, OH 45015
Tel: 513-896-7089
www.sugarcraft.com

Global Sugar Art
1509 Military Turnpike
Plattsburgh, NY 12901
Tel: 1-518-561-3039
Or: 1-800-420-6088
www.globalsugarart.com

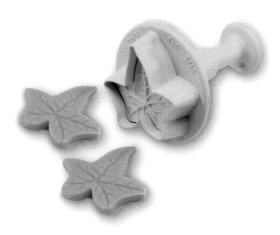

Index

Credits

I would like to thank the following companies for their help in providing material and equipment for use in this book:

Design-a-cake
30–31 Phoenix Road
Crowther Industrial Estate
Washington
Tyne and Wear
NE38 0AD
Tel: 0191 4177377
www.design-a-cake.co.uk

Luminati
The Display Works
East Way
Lee Mill Industrial Estate
Ivybridge
Devon
PL21 9GE
Tel: 01752 698720
www.cake-stands.co.uk

Renshaw
Crown Street
Liverpool
L8 7RF
Tel:0151 706 8200
www.renshaw-nbf.co.uk

Secret Ingredients
www.secret-ingredients.com

Squires Kitchen
3 Waverley Lane
Farnham
Surrey
GU9 8BB
Tel: 01252 260260
www.squires-shop.com

The Sugar Smith
5–6 Post Office Walk
Fore Street
Hertford
Hertfordshire
SG14 1DL
Tel:01992 500974
www.thesugarsmith.com

Many thanks to my cake show helpers: Georgina Adams, Cheryl Collin, Liz Fossey, Nicola Gill, Helen Gillingham, Vanessa Martin, Lone Perrotton, and Helen Williams.

Quarto would like to thank and acknowledge the following for their contribution to this book:

Alan Dunn, Dianne Gruenberg, Sheila Lampkin, Tracey Mann, and Helen Penman.

Images courtesy of iStockphotos, p.126–127
Images courtesy of Getty Images, p.91bl, 92l, 101bl, 106bl, 131, 136tl
Images courtesy of Shutterstock.com and the following photographers: Africa Studio, p.10bc; Amnartk, p.11bl; Arhelger, Tobias, p.102-103; Barbone, Marilyn, p.63br; Black, Ruth, pp.40-41, 88t, 88bl, 94t, 107cl, 113tr; Blais, Andre, p.113bl; Debono, Dennis, p.17tcr; ElenaGaak, p.134cr; Ericlefrancais, p.11cl; Ffolas, p.19br; Foodpictures, p.139t; GVictoria, p.17tr; Henriksson, Rose-Marie, p.93r; Hera, Jiri, p.139cl; Huls, Jenn, p.118bl; Jetrel, p.19bc; Kohlbacher, Timo, p.128t; Lynea, p.49br; Mayakova, p.96tl; Nui7711, pp.11bl, 23tr; Ozmen, M. Unal, p.129br; Pearl7, p.141b; Schweitzer, Elena, p.97b; Sutsaiy, pp.11cl, 23tr; Taliun, Diana, p.129bc; Tkacenko, Andris, p.106br; Trailexplorers, p.11tl ; VikaRayu, p.27tr

All other photographs and illustrations are the copyright of Quarto Publishing plc. While every effort has been made to credit contributors, Quarto would like to apologize should there have been any omissions or errors—and would be pleased to make the appropriate correction for future editions of the book.